HIDDEN
HANDEDNESS

The Emerging Story of Handedness Reversals

Published in cooperation with the Foundation For Handedness
Research

ISBN: 978-1-58939-966-2

Library of Congress Control Number: 2006939967

Dedicated to my wife, Tralee.

Whenever the struggle of birthing this book turned me into a high maintenance husband, I learned thankfully that I had <u>not</u> reached the limits of your patience or faith in what I had to accomplish. Your help was the wind in my sails that made this endeavor possible.

Acknowledgments

It is truly impossible to pin down the single person who can be blamed for the creation of this book, but Floyd Sichi and Oliver Sacks both qualify. Somehow, these two managed to convey their faith in what was possible to me. Their encouragement launched me into action.

My wife and family members have all lent me their steady support and strength. Each one has meant far more to me and to the successful completion of this project than they might suspect.

Thanks go to the circle of friends who took the time to express their interest in what I was attempting, and to follow my progress while offering their kind words of encouragement. Bob Joslin PE (who coined the term Lateral Lobotomy in a discussion regarding submergees) John Urrutia, Fred Fredette, LCSW, Scott Craig, Don Jordan, John and Heather Cameron, Mel Lee, and Brad Mazzoco of Focus On the Family. Each one of these friends has offered invaluable support.

My heartfelt appreciation is owed to those who were kind enough to read through drafts of the manuscript. To Marcia Jones, Alvin and Audrey Greenwald, Randy and Maggie Randolph, Dennis Gillen, PhD, Donald Gumm, DC, Cathy Price, Murray Renfrew, MD, Bill Stephens PhD, Rabbi Herb Opalek, PhD, Steve Pierce, Andy Tolsma, PhD, Rod and Rena Webster, John Cunningham, Nancy Brawley, Gene and Grace Luxon, Lane Luxon, DC, Bob and Nell Ohman, Alan and Colleen Croft. Liz Sabine, Literary Agent read the manuscript and offered important insights that helped to inspire the final editing process. Extra credit and three gold stars are hereby awarded to Terri Hall for her careful reading and insightful comments made the very end of the project.

Oliver Sacks, MD, Donald Joy PhD and Harold Levinson, MD are all owed a special note of thanks. However, Dawn L. Strongin, PhD, Associate Professor of Psychology at CSUS Stanislaus really deserves my deepest thanks. Dr. Strongin's labor of love in connection with this work included three successive, very detailed and thoughtful edits of the manuscript. Each of Dr. Strongin's responses were offered with warmth and patience blended with her unique humor which helped me to laugh and cry joyful tears each time she administered the "wounds" of a friend and a true professional. Without her insight, honesty, contributions of key research, and her persistent faith in the value of the project, this book would not have been possible.

I am certain that there are many others whose names should appear here as well. To you who also richly deserve to be thanked, I would like to express my gratitude for your help.

TABLE OF CONTENTS

INTRODUCTION

Hidden Handedness begins with a powerful discovery by one person who yearns to know if others have known such magic. In searching to answer that question, the really incredible discovery follows, the fact that the world is full of sleepers or "submergees" – people whose handedness was reversed at a young age. The premise of this book is that millions, perhaps 800 million people inhabiting the world today and many more who have lived out their lives in history are or have been marked by the special characteristics and behaviors of submergees.

An even more unusual finding is that a way home from submergee alienation exists. The pathway back is described through the eyes of a pioneer submergee who made the journey back and expects that others may choose to follow.

Hidden Handedness is written to unveil what has been unseen, a world populated by an undiscovered handedness group, one whose consciousness and talents have been altered. Some have changed history, but all have paid a price to conform to the handedness standards of others. Join in and discover what this world is about, a place of opportunity to learn and change for submergees, and for the rest, a chance to enter into a new world, one we have yet to name and yet to truly see.

TELLING THE SUBMERGEE STORY ~ CHAPTER 1

"Ah," he groaned, "Enchantments, enchantments . . . the heavy tangled, cold, clammy web of evil magic. Buried alive. Dragged down under the earth, down into the sooty blackness . . . how many years is it? . . . Have I lived ten years, or a thousand years in the pit? Maggot men all around me. Oh, have mercy. Let me out, let me go back. Let me feel the wind and see the sky . . . There used to be a little pool. When you looked down into it you could see all the trees growing upside down in the water, all green, and below them, deep, very deep, the blue sky." -- Prince Rillian

The Silver Chair - C.S. Lewis.

Drawing back the curtains and letting you, dear reader, into my life isn't easy, but it must be done. You see, I represent a special segment of humanity that needs to be discovered and understood. In order for that to happen, someone needs to share our story. You may call us "converted left-handers" or "converted right-handers", as some have, but I choose to use the term *submergee* to describe what I once was: a left-handed child who grew into adulthood thinking of himself as a right-hander. Now that I know the truth about my self, I live life as a left-hander and refer to myself as an *emergee*, a term that describes the person that I have become since returning to my native handedness.

Most of what I will share relates to submergees, a hidden group of humans whose handedness has been reversed. Submergees include left-handers whose handedness has been reversed, as well as right-handers who have been trained to become left-handed. From the ranks of these submergees, another large handedness group may be birthed: those submergees who choose to emerge--to return to their native handedness.

1

Submergees have the opportunity to emerge from their alien state of body and mind, one which keeps them estranged from the self they were born to be. However, it appears that submergees very rarely embark on the journey that enables them to become an emergee. I did. By telling my story, I hope to put an end to the silence that has kept this subject hidden from society and from the submergees that have been and continue to be created.

According to my parents, I began my descent into the submergee world sometime around my first birthday. My parents decided to train their left-handed boy to become a right-handed child. Little did they realize that re-routing a child's handedness also re-routes and rewires the brain. Modern insights into the plasticity, or malleable nature, of the developing human body and mind were still decades over the horizon when I was detoured onto the pathway that would lead me to become a submergee.

Insofar as I know, this book represents the first written account of what it was like to live as a submergee who chose to become an emergee. After learning at age forty-one that I wasn't a right-hander, I unwittingly opened the door of the cell I was trapped in by choosing to become left-handed again. In discovering that I had been set free, I began the journey of my lifetime. I will describe the process that took place as I left my submergee prison behind and began to walk down the pathway of recovery.

"A PIECE OF CAKE!"

I first became aware of my left-handed heritage while playing tennis on a Sunday afternoon, March 5, 1995. I'll share the details of how that happened later, but, based on what I knew at the time I made my discovery, it was reasonable to assume that a return to my native left-handedness would be a simple process, a piece of cake!

I thought it made perfect sense for a converted left or right-hander like me to do the logical and natural thing and return to his native handedness. However, after 40 years of living in an altered submergee state, I soon found that my body and mind had adapted

2

in ways I couldn't have begun to imagine. There are degrees of handedness and, as it turned out, I am strongly left-handed. My strong left-handedness meant that I was actually something of a human pretzel with billions of powerful twists and loops that needed to be unraveled. The fact that I was ignorant of what was about to happen left me completely unprepared for what lay ahead.

One of the first lessons I learned as a new emergee is that there is a pressing need for unique terms that can be used to describe the experience of living in a state of altered handedness, as well as the state that ensues when one returns to his or her native handedness. Assembled phrases have been pressed into service by others in an attempt to describe the unique submergee state. Unfortunately, borrowed phrases are subject to varying interpretations, depending on the context in which they are used, and on the reader's point of view. With a precise set of terms available to use, the task of writing about or discussing the topic of reversed handedness is greatly simplified. This special group or "tribe" of human beings deserves and in fact needs to have its own identity.

To simplify the discussion of *what* handedness is, I have adopted the convention that the hand one chooses to use for writing is the dominant hand. With the very rare exception of those whose handwriting is truly ambidextrous, the vast majority of humans choose to operate in an asymmetric pattern; writing almost exclusively with either the left or right hand.[1]

In addition to unique terms, it is valuable to have a picture of handedness that provides us with another perspective for discussion. In order to develop that picture, I have adopted a convention of five forms of handedness based on current views regarding the population of the first three handedness types.

Handedness Types

Numeric by population	Standard terms for groups	Group size
First hand	Right-handed	Largest group
Second hand	Left-handed	Second largest group
Third hand	Ambidextrous	Smallest group
Fourth hand	Submergees	Unknown
Fifth hand	Emergees	Unknown

Had it not been for the curious expressions evoked by the phrase, I would have named this book *The Fifth Hand* in order to help illustrate the importance that attaches to having two new handedness groups in society.

Working within a framework of five types of handedness, the First Hand is the largest group: right-handers. The Second Hand is the next largest handedness group: left-handers. The Third Hand is the group of individuals who are classified as ambidextrous. To the convention of three handedness types, I have added two more. The first addition is the Fourth Hand, made up of submergees, the group whose handedness has been reversed. The second addition is the Fifth Hand, composed of emergees, those who emerge from the ranks of submergees and return from their imposed handedness to their native handedness.

Having an expanded framework of five forms of handedness makes it possible to discuss the topic in a more complete and meaningful context. In time, improved understandings of handedness will no doubt require the use of more detailed categories, but for the moment, the convention of five types of handedness serves the purpose of unifying the two newer handedness groups of submergees and emergees with the existing groups of right, left and ambidextrous handedness that we are already familiar with.

For an example of how these five handedness groupings may be used, I would say of myself, *I began life as a left-handed child* (Second Hand). Starting at age one, submergee pressures were applied and I learned to live for forty years as a submergee (Fourth Hand). After living forty years as a member of the Fourth Hand group, I became an emergee by becoming a re-created left-hander, thereby becoming a member of the Fifth Hand.

Submergees are altered due to the *twisting* of body and mind that takes place in accommodating the massive functional shift that occurs when a permanent reversal of handedness occurs.[2] Contrary to what might otherwise seem intuitive, studies have shown that innate handedness preferences persist into adulthood despite the fact that submergee training typically takes place in the early developmental years. Submergees are neither left nor right-handed nor are they ambidextrous when living in their state of reversed handedness. What I refer to as a "limbo of identity" applies to both submergees and to those who choose to emerge. Once the submergee and emergee populations are in view, three terms we commonly use for handedness (left, right, and ambidextrous) fail to encompass the full scope of handedness. Both the person whose handedness is reversed and the one who returns from this state have developed into a state of handedness for which no name exists.[3]

To say that I simply became left-handed again or that I went back to become a member of the Second Hand group at age forty-one would be inappropriate because, to do so, I would have to assert that my forty year experience as a submergee neither reshaped nor had a lasting influence on my body and mind. The truth is that the experiences of my submergee past will forever influence and inform the person that I am today. The same can be said for the submergees who choose not to return, who decide that they wish to remain in their submergee state. Because submergees and emergees alike are forever altered by their changed state of body and mind, we need a means of acknowledging and understanding the unique identity and characteristics of each handedness group.

When comparing the events that create submergees and emergees, I have come to view the initial rewiring of the body and mind that takes place in a child who becomes a submergee as the more difficult process. The difference between becoming a submergee child and an emergee adult is that while a submergee must learn to overcome his or her innate laterality, the emergee simply sets it free. Although there are challenges in the process, the emergee adult learns to swim with and not against his body and mind's native currents of function and expression. The emergee in essence ceases the striving that it took to create and maintain the submergee state and this reversal enables the body and mind system to begin functioning as originally intended, in its most efficient manner.

Reversing one's innate laterality entails an override of programmed preferences that requires the kind of high-order plasticity or neural adaptability for which young children are noted. Submergee children in-the-making must learn to swim against the current of their innate handedness in order to reverse their dominant handedness. These children are learning to do something that is foreign to their nature. They must develop in a way that enables them to function in an operating environment they weren't intended to inhabit. The pliable nature of the young body and mind makes this profound revision or rewiring possible in spite of the high price in functionality that the child must pay.

In contrast to the adult emergee who chooses to cooperate with his or her built-in preferences for laterality and handedness, the submergee child has to somehow learn to resist and, in time, overcome these same forces. First, the submergee child must find a way to counteract his or her natural developmental guidance system; and, having achieved that unnatural feat, the child must invest the energy required to maintain his or her reversed operating state. This wholesale conversion of the original architecture of laterality represents a life-long alteration of neurology and function that impacts the available energy, gifts and talents of the submergee individual for the balance of their lives.

The extensive accommodations the submergee child must make in order to shift his or her handedness drive massive shifts in the operation of their body and mind. An emergee return is equally profound, because it must undo the many submergee adaptations that took place in childhood. In my view, it is the accelerated reversal or "undoing" of many years of juvenile adaptation that appears to make the emergee healing process such a dramatic event. If the plasticity of the young mind were compared to a spring, one could think of the body and mind of a submergee child as a very elastic spring that has been loaded with great force. An emergee return unleashes these accumulated forces that have been held in place by the unique form of resistance that is required to maintain the unnatural submergee state.

At present I divide submergees into two categories, *normal submergees* and *deep submergees*. Normal submergees are those individuals who can recall the memory of being trained or forced to become a submergee. If asked, normal submergees, such as author Jack Fincher, or my own father, can clearly remember those moments when the pressures to become right-handed were successfully applied by adults.

In contrast to normal submergees, deep submergees do not have access to the memories of their handedness reversal experiences. Using myself as an example, I was unaware of my submergee history. Until March 5, 1995, I would have laughed at anyone who suggested that I might actually be left-handed. As an adult whose submergee training began at approximately one year of age, I had no intact reference points to betray my left-handedness, no way to sense that something might be wrong. Only after unexpectedly discovering the truth about my heritage, and then seeing it with fresh eyes, did the first pieces of my puzzle begin to fall into place. I had to form my understanding of what had actually happened to me by first emerging and then working backwards in time in order to understand the real me. I came to see that I had been blinded by my own deep submergee mind-set combined with a total absence of public awareness that submergees existed.

When considering his handedness history, my father, who is a normal submergee, has always had a mental "whodunit" or historical reference point to which he can connect. He has clear memories of being forced not to use his left hand by his first-grade teacher. For example, he remembers being forced to use only his right hand when writing on the chalkboard. Normal submergees know the history of their handedness reversals, but they tend to view the events with limited understanding of the consequences that followed. It's not uncommon to hear normal submergees say *I was forced to switch handedness,* while in the same breath commenting, *Being switched was probably best for me anyhow.*

I am aware of a very limited amount of biographical material that has been written by submergees. The resources listed in the endnotes will provide the interested reader with these references.[4] In addition, a large body of biographical materials exists that documents the behavior of socially prominent submergees. The biographical window on submergees has proved to be a rich source of inspiration and insight to me in my studies, and it is one that I will refer to later. No doubt, the short list of pertinent books and materials to which one can refer will grow rapidly, once the topic of hidden handedness becomes a publicly recognized issue.

An important principle to keep in mind regarding handedness is the fact that each of us has his or her own unique set of innate preferences and characteristics. Each individual will respond differently if and when submergee pressures are applied at a young age or when an emergee process is initiated at a later date. These differences are captured nicely by the concept of rating "strengths of handedness" on a graded scale as Marian Annette does in recognizing variations in handedness.[5] In my case, I am strongly left-handed, and I lived as a deep submergee. For this reason, my experience of both the deficits of the submergee state and the benefits of the emergee process was a powerful one. Based on Annette's model, it stands to reason that submergees and emergees will have experiences that will vary depending upon their individual makeup.

Viewing my submergee past with the clarity of hindsight, it is clear that living as a left-hander is so much easier, faster, and more complete than living as a submergee that the old operating state seems almost like that of a zombie. While "zombie" might seem like an extreme characterization, I would now say that I once lived and moved through life as if I was a shadow of myself, a semblance of the real me.

As a submergee, I was fully convinced that I was right-handed. I automatically edited my perceptions of self, assuming that all skilled tasks should be done with the right hand. I am still amazed by the manner in which my mind had learned to edit reality in accord with my adopted suppositions about my handedness. While I can't speak for other submergees, it is possible that my case is extreme, because I am both strongly left-handed and was a deep submergee. My emergee experiences, and the insights that resulted from them, created a sharp set of contrasts on the subject of submergees, one seen from within and one from without. Having lived through the emergee experience, I am regularly inspired as I consider the contrasting perspectives that are at work in the world of the submergee and the emergee.

My submergee father is less strongly inclined to left-handedness than I am. His strength of handedness places him closer to the central axis of handedness (ambidexterity) than me. His more "balanced" state of handedness seems to have enabled him to adapt to his submergee state with less difficulty. While he shares many of the special personality traits I have learned to associate with persons who are submergees, he is a good athlete, and did not suffer from learning disabilities to the degree that I did. Like the majority of submergees, he prefers to print rather than use cursive handwriting, but he has a flowing cursive script when signing his name. It appears as if his submergee rewiring was less disruptive or costly because his preference or strength of handedness is not as strong as mine.

I am looking forward to the years ahead, when submergees begin to share their stories. As we start to learn how these individuals have shaped and are now shaping history, their stories will bring meaning to this heretofore hidden aspect of human handedness in ways that we can only begin to imagine.

OUR FAMILY SETTING ~ CHAPTER 2

During a visit from Samuel's grandmother, when he was just about a year old and beginning to feed himself with his little fork, she noticed that he was using his left hand and became very concerned. She herself was very strongly left-handed, but had found that the world was made for right-handed people. So she took the fork from his left hand and said to me, his mother, 'Begin putting everything in his right hand now and he'll learn early to adjust.'

I can't remember that we made any big program of this. Samuel was of a very sweet nature and was a child who wanted to please his Mother and Father, and his big brother, Bob. He may have watched his right-handed brother and father as they threw balls or stacked blocks and thought, 'O.K. I'll do it that way.'

He was found to be dyslexic in second grade and was given extra help with reading. Because he was very bright, he seemed to be doing all right. It never occurred to us to connect the dyslexic problem with his early preference for his left hand.

Margaret M. Randolph -- July 15, 2003

My oldest brother was born in 1950. I was born a few years later, the middle child in a family of three sons. We are fortunate to have a mother and father who love us dearly, and we are further blessed by the fact that all five members of the family are alive and well. We are part of the generation of children whose parents grew up during the depression and came of age at the height of World War II. In this context, the meaning of words like "winner" or "loser" had a special significance that was not lost on my parents.

The pertinent details were in place for the creation of a submergee child; right time, right place, right parents and right grandmother.

All that was needed was the birth of a left-handed son.

My paternal grandmother was born in Beaumont, Texas. She married my grandfather, born in Huntsville Texas. Grandmother Randolph was strongly left-handed and remained left-handed for life. She bitterly regretted the fact that she had been born with what she referred to as the "curse of left-handedness." An example of her left-handed signature shows how she put forth a strong effort to maintain a right-handed slant (see Figure 1).

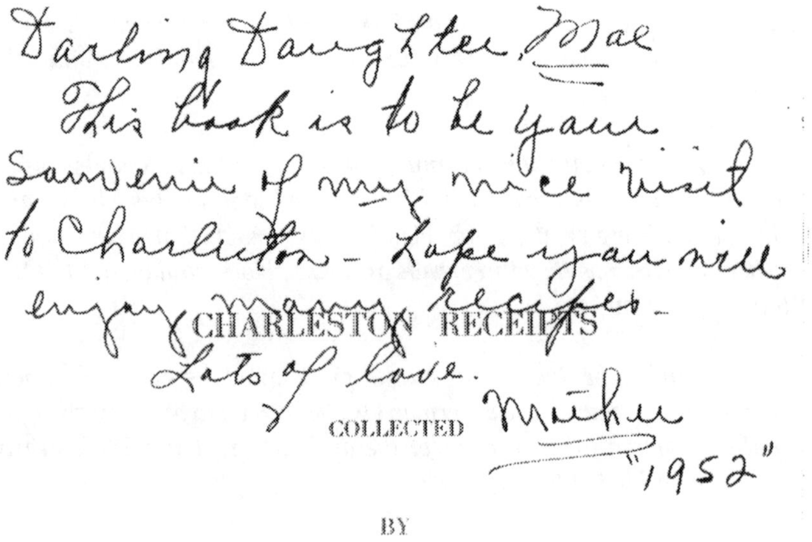

Figure 1.

When I first saw Grandmother's handwriting and signature, after I had become an emergee, I was deeply moved by the struggle that was evident as she tried to make her handwriting look like the product of a right-handed writer. Her signature and family stories reveal that she experienced significant shame over her left-handedness. My father's stories make it clear that Grandmother dearly wished she could have been born right-handed. One of her greatest struggles resulted from the fact that she owned and operated a hair salon and had no choice but to use the only scissors available at that time. Forced to cut hair with right-handed scissors, she was reminded constantly that left-handed people had to pay a steep price for their abnormality. The hair cutting torture added insult to the primary injury of being an outsider

Grandmother's era was a time when left-handers were regarded as inferior or even evil by most of society. A wonderful children's book written in the days of Babe Ruth by author John H. Ritter, provides readers with important insights into the social pressures that Grandmother faced. *Choosing Up Sides* is told through the eyes of Luke, a left-handed boy who is rejected by his father when against his father's wishes, he decides to put his outstanding left-handed pitching skills to good use. Ritter's book is an entertaining read for those who would like to learn about the trials of left-handers living in the days of the great submergee baseball player, Babe Ruth.

Grandmother became convinced that a lefty who learned to become right-handed would have a far better life than one who had to go through life struggling with his or her left-handedness, as she had. After all, by the time I was born, my submergee father had been living successfully as a right-handed person for more than twenty-five years and he had earned a degree in Mechanical Engineering. She had no reason to doubt that submergees could succeed in the world because her son's life experiences demonstrated the wisdom of her decision to support his transition to submergee status at an early age.

Returning to my early years in school, while I have many pleasant memories of kindergarten experiences, no memories remain intact from the first grade, when a much less pleasant set of experiences began. I do know that I didn't succeed academically in first grade. My mother reports that there were serious questions about holding me back for an additional year in first grade due to these struggles. The question was complicated by the fact that I had entered kindergarten at age four, earlier than most children. Because of my academic deficits, my early school experiences were characterized by shame, accompanied by negative internal and external feedback.

I am leaving out the details of the "culprit" first grade teacher since my memory of this year in school is still a total blank. Regardless of what happened or didn't happen to me in the first grade classroom, by second grade, the transfer to a right-handed mode of function was almost complete (see figure 2). Over time, my struggle only grew more and more pronounced (see figure 3).

Kindergarten   Second Grade

Figure 2.

Family films and pictures of me from the first grade forward show a child with a sunny disposition who keeps squinting and closing his left eye. I have memories from second-grade classroom writing experiences in which I would consistently twist my head around to the left while printing on the paper. As I wrote, I would keep the paper within a few inches of my right eye as I gazed down at the paper from that side of my face. Apparently, I assumed this contorted posture when writing so I could look at the paper sideways, enabling me to keep my left eye disconnected from the task at hand while my right eye remained focused on the work of my right hand.

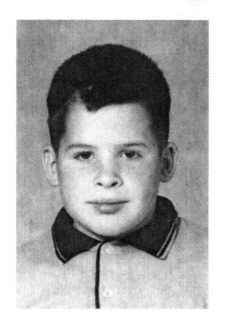 

Third grade   Fourth grade

Figure 3.

The growing inner sense of loneliness, humiliation, frustration and hopelessness I felt as I struggled in school are very difficult to convey accurately. The difference in life experiences I have written about is reflected in the eyes and expressions captured by the third and fourth grade photographs. Along with the increasing frustration I felt as I fought to overcome submergee deficits came a nagging inner sense that I was deeply flawed. The seeds that would eventually sprout and grow into an ongoing battle with depression began to take root within me.

On Monday, when the sun is hot
I wonder to myself a lot:
'Now is it true, or is it not,
'That what is which and which is what?'

Winnie-the-Pooh - A.A. Milne

Stories help us to travel in many ways -- through time, the eyes of others and even to various vantage points that enable us to see a single experience from different perspectives. In order to understand submergee children better, I would like to share the stories of a young submergee, introducing you to the world as I saw it, not so long ago.

Remember - Remembering the day

I am five years old and I am sitting cross-legged on the concrete patio behind our home. I am facing east, with my back to the house, looking out on the lawn and play area of our back yard. Something has happened and I am very sad. I hold the palm of my left hand up close to my face, looking at it carefully with my left eye. To me, my left palm looks like the face of a dear friend who I have lost forever. I gaze at the lines running across the skin and, as I do, I slowly and deliberately repeat out loud to myself *remember...* *remember . . . remember.* I can recall doing this on at least three separate occasions, always in the same place and in the same manner.

Many years later I can recall this strange ritual and get a haunting feeling inside every time I relive the moment. Those repeated words were a farewell, perhaps to the real me. They were all I would have to hang on to -- like the advice of a dearly departed

16

friend. The words were spoken to the part of me that would have to get by, to live out a prison sentence of submergee existence that would endure for forty years. Eventually I would hear the advice again in memory, and this time the meaning would be clear, when the one who had spoken them returned to life many years later.

Remembering the night

I am five-years-old and in the midst of a dream. My older brother is asleep, resting in the upper level of the bunk bed that we share. Outside, the lightning bolts from a winter storm make cracking and booming sounds in the wind of a moonless night.

We are sleeping in the upstairs bedroom of our home. If it wasn't so dark, you could have seen the top of the staircase on the north side of the room. A small door to the south opens into an unfinished attic. Behind that door, a brick chimney rises from the living room hearth below and up through the roof above. Tonight, the exposed part of the chimney is wet with rain, its brick surface acts like the prow of a small boat, parting the foaming gusts of wind.

I am lying on my back with my feet facing the door to the unfinished attic. In this position, the chimney is located slightly to my left. The flash of lightning and the sound of thunder come closer and closer as the fury of the storm increases. I am fearful that our home will not be strong enough to withstand this storm. It could be blown apart by a gust of wind, or set on fire by a bolt of lightening. Suddenly I see a yellow bolt of energy leaping down upon our home. Rushing through the chimney flue and across the floor, it reaches my feet before I can move. The angry sound of thunder fills the small room and muffles my cries for help. No one hears me. The sharp fingertips of electricity have me in their crackling grip. My body is jerking beyond my control as the lightning bolt snaps at me.

I don't know if I will survive this attack. As each new bolt grabs me, I see the room lit brightly by the glare of the yellow force. For a brief moment, the room grows dark and quiet, but I remain speechless, frozen in shock, barely able to breathe. Another high voltage bolt reaches down and finds its way into the room. The force of this attack is beyond understanding and now I am wondering if I will die. I am in one of my worst nightmares ever, and awaken suddenly, screaming in terror.

This dream happens only once, but it remains one of my most vivid memories.

The "ABC Song"

September 1956. The first day of kindergarten.

I am four years old and anxiously sitting in the front passenger seat of our car because it is the first day of school. The car is parked in front of the school and Mom is seated next to me, at the wheel. She is dropping me off to start kindergarten and I am eager to get going. We can see the playground and the kindergarten classroom through the windshield.

Mom says, *Now, Sam, I want you to sing your alphabet for me.* I begin at A, using the song she taught me so I can make it from beginning to end. As I sing, I manage to get all the way to the letter P, but then I stumble on *Q...R...S...T....* I can't make it all the way to the end! The song isn't working right.

As soon as I realize that I have failed to say my alphabet, all of the letters start to spin around inside of me. They are out of control, going everywhere. I feel desperate and wonder if Mom will ever let me go to school. I am sure that, unless I finish the alphabet for her, I will never get to go to school. I try again and fail twice more, feeling more ashamed each time. School is supposed to be fun, but something is wrong with me.

Pencil

I am five years old and it is some time just after breakfast. Mom has me seated on a barstool, facing the kitchen, so I can write on the counter top. She is standing next to me, on my left side. In my right hand, I hold a yellow pencil, just like the kind we use in school. I can barely hold the pencil because my right arm and hand are too weak to do the job. It feels like something is wrong with my hand. It feels like it is numb or half-asleep and I can't wake it up. I am worried that my hand is so weak that I will drop the pencil, because it feels so awkward and hard to hold. I don't have the strength to hold the yellow pencil with a grip that is firm enough to write.

I try to push the pencil onto the lined paper, but I cannot develop enough pressure to write properly. I find that it takes lots of pressure to leave marks on the paper with the pencil, and I just cannot get my fingers or the muscles in my hand and forearm working well enough to make marks, let alone letters. I am paralyzed, like I had just hit the funny bone in my right elbow. Trying harder to write makes the sense of helplessness grow worse. The pencil seems like a tree and I am some kind of a worm wiggling at the roots. *I* am blushing with embarrassment, feeling hot and ashamed inside.

I am in a state of shock, or at least my hand is, but when Mom sees my struggle with the pencil she says to me in a firm voice, *Write!* Her encouragement only makes the problem worse. Now my hand feels even weaker than before. As the moments pass, I grow more ashamed and helpless, wondering *What's wrong with my hand? What's wrong with me?*

Compensate

It's summertime at the beach, just after noon. The salty smell of an offshore breeze is blowing across my suntanned skin. I am six years old, standing in the wet sand and gazing out on the vastness of the Pacific Ocean.

The ankle-deep surf rushes up and down around my feet. There's a dreamy quality about the scene. I come here often when I am asleep. I turn around with my back to the waves so I can move higher up. As I begin to move uphill, I look down and see my feet on the wet sand. The sand looks like a perfectly flat mirror that has a shiny film of clear water with flecks of bubbly white foam moving over its surface. The sand stays still but, as I watch, I can see that the water is starting to move down, back toward the ocean.

As I start to run, the moving water slows my progress. The water rushes madly backwards, toward the waves. I look down again as the water accelerates, going faster and faster, grabbing my ankles and sucking the sand out from under the soles of my feet. I find that I must shift my weight to keep from losing my balance. My stomach feels as if a large hand is pressing against it, pushing me away from the beach and toward the ocean. I lean uphill and try to run harder, taking huge strides in order to overcome the forces that I am fighting against. In my mind's eye, I can see that each step I take is measured against a surface of moving water and time, that is all headed in the opposite direction, into the ocean. I want to move forward, but I am stuck in one place and my legs feel like wax. I fight against a growing sense of despair, because I can't get anywhere even though I am trying with all my strength to run uphill. I am not strong enough or fast enough to overcome the moving world of sand and water.

For many years this dream recurs. I am always too slow and never strong enough to overcome the forces on the surface of the moving mirror. The water clutches at me endlessly and its sandy grip cannot be broken.

Compensate ~ The Magic Shirt and Shoes

I am in my third-grade classroom, right after morning recess. I am feeling lucky today, because I am wearing my magic shirt and shoes. My very favorite shirt is a gold knit with short sleeves. It has a black collar and black pin stripes at the ends of the sleeves. There is an embroidered emblem of two lions facing each other stitched into the left breast pocket that looks just like a knight's crest. The lions are embroidered in with black and they are standing up on their hind legs with their claws stretched out and their jaws wide open in a roar! My shoes are made of brown leather with thick rubber soles that make me want to run. Whenever I wear my magic shirt together with my special brown shoes, I can run faster and farther than anybody else on the playground because they help me to take extra-long super strides.

During recess today, my magic shirt and special shoes helped me to zoom across the ground as if my shoes had wings! On a day like this, I can float above the ground if I want to. I feel safe and smart. I remind myself that I have super powers today, that I have the power to fly and to run as far and as fast as I want to, whenever I want to, which makes playing games like kick ball way more fun. It is as if I am wearing the magic cape and ring of a super hero, except no one can tell that I have them on.

Along the full length of one classroom wall, our teacher has placed little rocket-shaped cutouts of colored paper with our names written on them. Every time we finish a book, we turn in our report and the teacher makes our space ship fly one step closer to its destination. Once your rocket crosses the finish line, the teacher gives you your very own book to take home as a reward. I like reading, so my ship is keeping up with most of the other kids in class.

Writing, spelling and arithmetic are different though, and now it is time to write. *Oh-oh!* I think. I start to write with my right hand. I twist my head way around to the left, and lean hard over the paper so I can get my right eye as close to the point of the pencil as possible. Whenever I write like this, my left eye can't see what my right hand is doing. Suddenly, I feel that I am standing in the surf again, with the shining mirror of foamy water moving downhill, shifting the sand under my feet. I am holding the pencil tightly with my right hand, but my feet begin to slip as the rushing water of the mirror fills my mind and I grow nauseous. I can hold the yellow pencil and make big printed letters, but the lines I make look like wet, wiggly spaghetti noodles. That's hard enough, but the real trouble comes when it is time to spell with those squiggly letters, or to add and subtract using squiggly numbers like I will have to do in a little while.

After school, Mom asks to see my work. She is not pleased with my arithmetic, my spelling or my writing. Then Mom picks up my papers and asks me to follow her as she walks to the mirror. *Now Sam, I want to show you something.* She holds the lined paper up to the mirror and asks me to read the paper by looking at it in the mirror. I can read the writing in the mirror just fine. Then Mom holds the paper up for me, so I can see it without viewing it in the mirror, and I can't read my own handwriting!

Wow! I think to myself. *What is this all about?* Mom doesn't understand it either, and I can tell she is worried about what this might mean. After I am tested by the eye doctor, Mom says that according to the doctor, there is something wrong with my eyes. He tells her that I have a lazy right eye.

After seeing the eye doctor, Mom begins working with me every day, using flash cards for math problems, and spelling. We also work on my handwriting. I know that my Mom and my Teacher are expecting me to find ways to be faster and more successful at school. I am not doing as well as they know I can do and they are both disappointed in me. I need to find a better way to move my body and mind. I need to move further up on the beach, to reach a place where the moving sand and dizzying mirror won't slow me down so much.

Eventually, I will learn to use the secret power of my magic shirt and special shoes to outrun the moving mirror all the time and make my way to higher ground in real life. These struggles will make me a different person - sadder, but also stronger. But every time I return to my dream on the beach, I am never fast or strong enough to escape. In that dream, I can never compensate enough.

Losing My Tickets and Finding God

It is a cool morning in early October. I am ten-years-old and bicycling to school by myself. As I ride, the tickets I have to sell for our Boy Scout Troop's steak dinner are in my thoughts: *I was issued $60.00 worth of tickets, but where are they now? I must have lost them!* Because I already lose track of everything, this thought that I have just lost something valuable hits my stomach like a drink of hot pickle juice. I feel sick, alone, embarrassed and lost. On the rest of the ride, I cry out internally, praying to God and hoping that He will understand my problem and do something about it! I have no idea what happened to those tickets. *$60.00! Man, that's a lot of money to lose! What's going to happen to me now, and how will I ever explain what happened to my dad?*

I lock my bike up and trudge into Mrs. Key's fifth-grade classroom. I am feeling like a lost sheep, alone, with no one to save me from the howling wolves. I ruminate, *Who would care for a sheep that just lost $60.00 in tickets?* After class has begun, an office assistant delivers a note to the teacher. After a moment, Mrs. Key calls my name. When I go up to her desk, she asks that I report to the principal's office immediately. I am generally a well-behaved boy, but I have a healthy respect for the principal, because of the stories I've heard about the big wooden paddle he uses to put bad boys back in line. I have no idea what he wants, but I dutifully plod along the silent corridor, alone. As I walk, my head spins while my stomach churns to keep it company.

The smell of floor wax in the hallway is swept away by the scent of paper and perfume in the reception area of the principal's office. The secretary greets me and asks me to take a seat while she lets the principal know that I have arrived. As I sit nervously on the wood bench, I look up at the school clock, which I notice, looks exactly like the one on the wall of our classroom. The black hands move over the black numbers on the white face the same way too, making a loud clunking sound with each minute that passes. Neither the fear of the principal nor the comparison of clocks can keep the thought of those tickets out of my mind. I keep wondering *where* they went and hating myself. *Why, why weren't you more careful with those expensive tickets?*

The secretary shows me into the principal's office. He is a big man. As he looks at me he says with a concerned voice, *Sam, we think we may have found some tickets that belong to you. I wanted to make sure you got them back right away, because they are worth a lot of money. I bet you were really worried about them.* He hands me the whole book of tickets. I open up the orange cover and count them. Not one ticket is missing! I hear him say, *You must have dropped them on the playground yesterday, because that is where they were found. One of our students turned them in this morning.*

I can't believe it! The agonizing load of shame I have been carrying is suddenly lifted. I no longer have to face the prospect of more shame and guilt. *Hooray, hooray for today!* I think joyfully as I thank the principal and leave his office with a great big smile. I fly past the secretary, a thankful fifth grader, clutching my precious ticket book tightly. The deep gloom that had enveloped me just moments before is annihilated by joy, a sense that the world is not such a horrible place after all.

A small seed of faith was planted deep in the soil of my heart that afternoon. I wasn't alone after all! What I had most dearly hoped for when I first cried out in despair was that I wasn't alone, that God could hear me after all. I'd had the intuition that God was real before, but this was the first time I had the chance to put it to the test. I found far more than a book of tickets that day.

BECOMING AN EMERGEE ~ CHAPTER 4

INCREDIBLE! My son, Samuel, is now an 'emergee' after living as a 'submergee' for 40 years--that is, he lived as a right-handed person, suffering learning disabilities, dyslexia and other trauma before he discovered that he indeed was a natural left-handed person and was courageous enough to embark on a journey of change. He started the process by copying the Book of Hebrews using his left hand, and moved on from that starting point. It has not been easy--very difficult--for his darling wife, Tralee. It has been difficult in oh so many ways, but he has persisted in his crusade and feels compelled to share this saga with others. I urge you to read his book; it could change your life.

George Binford Randolph - May 26, 2003

As I grew older, I gradually learned to compensate for many of my academic handicaps, my physical and social awkwardness, as well as my inner anxieties and insecurities. I matured physically (see figure 4) becoming strong and well coordinated. I gradually learned to behave in accord with the expected social graces but, inside, I felt that I had only learned to be a make-believe person, a false self, who held up a mask to convince others that I was confident and capable. I struggled to maintain my sense of personal value and poise in the face of a clear inner understanding that I could not measure up to either my own internal or external social standards.

By age sixteen, I had begun to learn how to "pass muster" and "fit in" to the world I lived in. My early physical awkwardness kept me from participating fully in team sports and other activities that required fine motor coordination and timing such as basketball and golf, or playing musical instruments, and dancing with a partner. As I grew stronger physically, I found that I was a fairly good distance runner, and I finally mastered the art of throwing a baseball long distances at the age of seventeen. I also earned a place on my high school's tennis team in my sophomore and junior years, playing as a member of a doubles team. In each case, my enthusiasm and drive helped to compensate for limited coordination and athletic skills.

High School

Figure 4.

As in sports, I struggled to overcome the academic deficits that resulted from my submergee wiring. After high school, I attended two four year universities, but struggled in both cases, falling back to earn an Associate of Arts degree from a community college. I earned 170 college credits, which would have qualified for an undergraduate degree in Construction Management, my primary field of study. Later college course work completed as an emergee has been a completely different experience as I have earned straight "A's" in all courses taken, including logic, physics and English.

I found my first real job working as a heavy equipment mechanic and later, manager of the same shop. I moved on to the roles of estimator and then manager of a general engineering construction firm and subsequently operated as an independent real estate appraiser. I am currently Vice President of a marketing firm, where I work together with members of my family.

In 1985, I read the book *Smart But Feeling Dumb* by Harold N. Levinson, M.D. As I read Levinson's book, I was struck by the manner in which many of the narratives of Levinson's patients paralleled my own experiences. For the first time in my life, I was introduced to people whose hidden difficulties and inner struggles were very much like my own. After much thought, I came to the conclusion that I must be a person who had simply learned to compensate for dyslexic handicaps. I finally had an appreciation for the hurdles I had to overcome every day of my life and I began to refer to myself as a "compensated dyslexic."

Thanks to Levinson's work, I had found a meaningful reference point to work from, recognizing and labeling numerous behaviors that were "unique to me" and for the first time, linking them to my struggle with dyslexia. I came to understand that the form of "dyslexia" I had meant that along with my academic deficits, I also had to struggle to distinguish individual voices from one another in noisy public settings or to accurately decipher the words of singers. I realized that when I became tired, my struggle to hear accurately became more acute. Once I understood that I was compensating for disabilities, I began to see how they were impacting my life. Of course, I couldn't appreciate the full range and depth of my deficits at the time, because I had no means of comparing my perceptions with those of a normal, unaffected person.

With the fresh insight that I had been compensating for hidden handicaps came the ability to love and accept myself *as is* for the very first time. What a profound relief! I belonged to a group of people known as dyslexics. Gaining this connection to others meant that my internal battles against shame and condemnation were something that I had in common with millions of others. My new awareness meant that I understood that I wasn't lazy or stupid. Levinson pointed out in *Smart But Feeling Dumb* that, contrary to the beliefs of many people most dyslexics are smart, innovative and hard-working individuals who feel as if they are dumb. Despite the fact that I worked harder than most to succeed, I too had struggled against the feeling that I was dumb. Levinson's book gave me my first hope that there might be a way out of the miry swamp in which I was trapped.

THE STORY SHIFTS GEARS

My emergee story started with a time of prayer that took place sometime early in January of 1995. While I don't have the exact date and time recorded, I can clearly recall being seated at my favorite spot for prayer and study when an internal conversation took place that day. I felt the need to come to grips with what I understood about my "compensated dyslexia" and the unique problems I faced. The prayer went something like this: *Lord, I know that I am struggling with disabilities, but why do I need to live like this? Do I really have to remain in a handicapped state for the rest of my life?* After some time passed, I received the distinct impression that somehow, God's purposes were being served by the very deficits I had to work so hard to overcome.

After thinking over the unexpected answer I received to my prayer, I realized that if my battles had a meaningful purpose, that purpose was sufficient reason for me to accept the difficulties willingly. I left my time of prayer thinking *Okay God, if it's Your will for me to remain disabled in this manner, even if I don't understand the details of your plan, I'm prepared to live out my life the way I am now, because I have your assurance that I'm Okay, as-is.*

Some two months would pass before the echo produced in that time of acceptance would come bouncing back into my life. I arrived at the pivotal moment of truth in my emergee story one

Hidden Handedness

Sunday afternoon while playing tennis. On March 5, 1995 I first realized that I was left-handed. The following narrative that I shared with a group of school counselors gives the details of that moment.

Two months later [after my time of prayer] *on a Sunday afternoon, March 5, 1995, my mind was inspired in a unique manner. Some have said of similar experiences, that the 'eyes of their understanding' were suddenly opened. The moment came for me as I was alone, practicing tennis against a backboard. While I moved back and forth to meet the ball, my tennis shoes made loud squeaking sounds on the concrete. I wasn't playing well, so in frustration I switched the racket to my left hand and continued to play. As I played left-handed, I noticed that I was moving more efficiently to meet the ball. It suddenly dawned on me that the squeaks I heard my shoes make while playing right-handed were clearly less organized than the squeaks made while playing left-handed. In one case there was a regular pattern of squeaks whereas the other pattern was disorganized and random. Hearing that difference, I suddenly just 'knew' that I was a lefty.*

As I think back on that moment when the light went on in my mind, I have to acknowledge God's mercy for the manner in which this 'Ah Ha!' experience happened. At that time, I would have rejected any one else's suggestion that I was really left-handed. Instead, I stumbled upon the clue that opened my eyes to the truth on my own. My suspicions were immediately affirmed, first by my wife, who had heard comments about reversed left-handers on a Focus On the Family radio program with Dr. Donald Joy. Finally, I called my parents to ask them about my history and both of them confirmed my suspicions. Mom explained that they had started training me to become right-handed when I was about one year old. She told me the story of Grandmother Randolph's early observations that I was left-handed and her recommendation to reverse my handedness, which they had followed.

If I really was left-handed, it seemed as if there was no option but to become the person I had been born to be. I had no idea of the 'mega changes' I was about to unleash by making this simple choice. I thought, this change might take a few minor adjustments but nothing major. Without realizing it, I was actually pulling the cork out of the bottle that had kept me trapped in my reversed handedness.

I TAKE MY FIRST STEPS AS AN EMERGEE

Once I discovered that I had been born left-handed, I did what seemed to be the most natural thing for me to do. If I was meant to be left-handed, why not go back to being what I was born to be? At the time that I made it, the decision to shift back to my innate left-handedness seemed rather trivial. To me, the question was like asking which of two small white economy cars I would prefer to drive. Brand A is almost identical to Brand B. When exchanging one such car for the other, one would see a few minor changes like a different cup holder and slightly different controls. Not (yawn) much of a difference, right? On the assumption that I was making a simple choice, I set forth to become left-handed.

Like any good story, this emergee tale takes off at the very moment when our hero falls asleep unsuspectingly in the middle of the deep dark magic forest, after eating a good meal. In my case, I had no idea what was going to happen as I began to retrain myself to be left-handed. For me, the critical moment arrived when I deliberately wrote my first lines using my left hand, coupled with the awareness that *This is it! I am finally doing what I was born to do, writing with my left hand!* (see Figures 5 and 6).

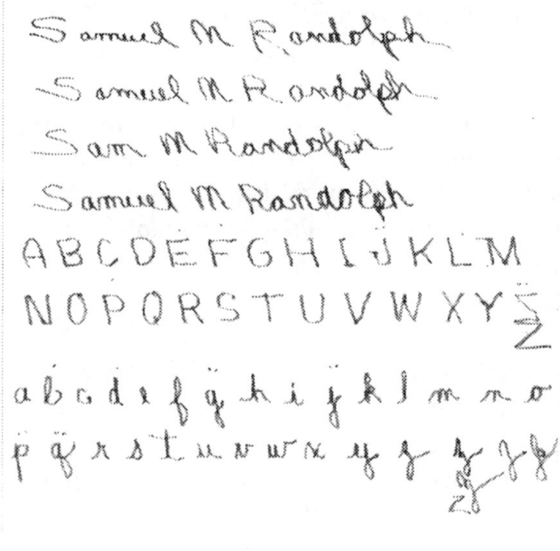
Samuel M Randolph
Samuel M Randolph
Sam M Randolph
Samuel M Randolph
ABCDEFGHIJKLM
NOPQRSTUVWXYZ

Figure 5.

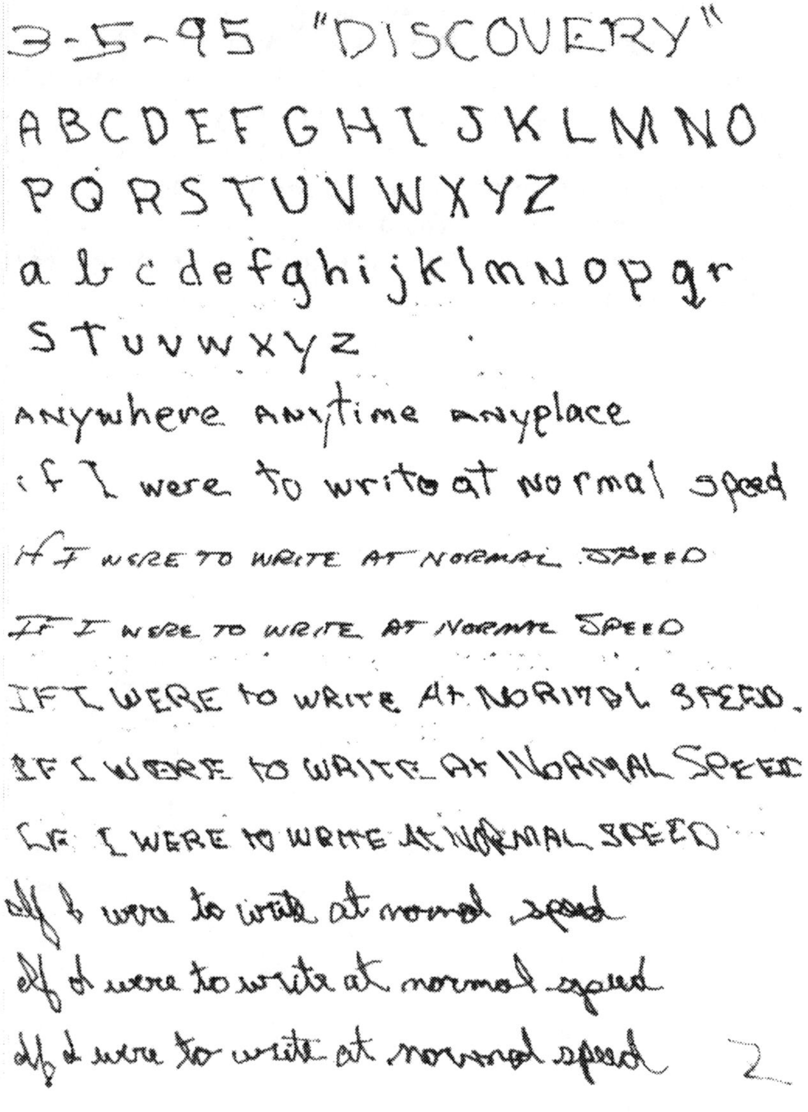

Figure 6.

Having read Harold Levinson's book *Smart But Feeling Dumb*, I "knew" that I was a "compensated dyslexic." But now, without understanding the power of change that existed within, I gripped a pen in my left hand and began to write. With pen in hand, and the knowledge that I was truly left-handed, I turned the key that finally unlocked and opened the submergee door. This was my moment of liberation. Once I began to live as a left-hander, my revised behaviors inexorably led me out of my submergee prison and into a new world of freedom. In the same way that migratory animals begin their journey from one hemisphere to the other with the flap of a wing or wave of a fluke, I began my own migration. I began journeying further and further from my submergee prison with each fresh stroke of the pen.

THE RETURN OF THE TRUE KING -- A SUBMERGEE FABLE ~ CHAPTER 5

I cannot rest from travel; I will drink life to the lees.
I am part of all that I have met; yet all experience
is an arch where through gleams that untraveled world
whose margin fades forever and forever when I move.
How dull it is to pause, to make an end, to rest unburnished,
Not to shine in use! As though to breathe were life!
Life piled on life were all too little, and of one to me little
remains; but every hour is saved from that eternal silence,
something more, a bringer of new things; and vile it were, for
some three suns to store and hoard myself, and this gray spirit
yearning in desire to follow knowledge like a sinking star
beyond the utmost bound of human thought

Excerpted from *Ulysses* - Alfred, Lord Tennyson

Once upon a time there was a fair city set within the Realm of Nyle, known as the City of Trundle. Alas, for the citizens of Trundle, the city which was once a fair and pleasant home for many, has fallen on hard times. Today, the citizens are living beneath a dark shadow of poverty that never lifts. Sir Steven, the Steward of Trundle, is severely vexed by the city's plight, because he and his counselors continue to find that they are powerless to reverse the fortunes of the city, to help the good citizens of Trundle break free from the dark sadness that has the city in its grip. The Steward is a good-hearted man with the best of intentions. He and his counselors believe that there must be a solution to the city's problems; yet year after year, the answers are not found. They believe a riddle must be solved before the city can regain its former glory, but the answer remains just out of reach and the city seems hopelessly lost in unending gloom.

Trundle rests on the banks of a broad river that flows smoothly through a once fertile valley. Many years ago, the Realm of Nyle and its cities were efficiently ruled by a powerful and capable king. Now, however, Nyle is in disarray and life is both difficult and dangerous throughout the Realm. The weather has changed for the worse; wind, clouds and heavy rains are common, while warm sunny days are rare. The rich green crops that once sprang from the fertile soils of the valley routinely fail. Crime, violence and lawlessness are rampant. The people have become demoralized by the constant struggle to survive, while their hunger for security and sufficiency grows. Even though the good people who live in the City of Trundle work hard, the days of plenty they once enjoyed have become faded memories.

A full generation has passed since the Kingdom and its cities were prosperous. To the shame of those who remember that past, present circumstances appear as a dark shadow compared to the bright days that once were common. For those who still have these memories, it is as if they are looking upward from the bottom of a deep pool of water, gazing up above the water's surface, and into the open air beyond. In memory, they can see the sun traveling freely through the blue sky above the water's smooth surface. A sense of sadness covers Trundle like a watery blanket that shadows and smothers everything. If only this burden could be taken away, the skies above Trundle would be filled with warm sunshine and soft breezes by day, and bright shining stars at night!

Occasionally, news arrives from the Realm of True, which is situated south of Nyle. The merchants of True are prosperous, but their ships rarely land in the ports of Nyle because its harbors are abandoned and its ports are overrun by crime.

The people of the Realm of True are blessed by the sovereign rule and administrative gifts of King Chauntly. Unfortunately, the prosperity of True is of little help to those living in the City of Trundle, except for a few youthful citizens. The talented youth of Trundle, rather than stay and inspire others, are instead drawn away to find success in the Realm of True, where they can prosper and raise their own families without fear.

As the sun is setting on the city, Sir Steven and his counselor, Sir Albert are enjoying a quiet dinner with Nyle's court recorder and historian, Drindle Foos. Sir Steven is seated at the head of the table, bent over from the weight of his deep concern for Trundle. He looks ten years older than his true age of forty-one. Steven gazes in a distracted manner at his two companions who, having served both his parents before him, are both a full generation older than he. *Sir Albert and Drindle Foos, please tell me about our past, tell me something of the history of the City of Trundle and the Realm of Nyle before the darkness descended* says Steven. *Tell me what went wrong and how it is that our fair Realm has fallen so far.*

Drindle Foos and Sir Albert exchange anxious glances, hesitating to see who will speak first. Finally, fulfilling his charge as the court historian, Drindle Foos begins to respond. He slowly unfolds the painful and seldom told history of Sir Steven's family, the Maxwells:

More than forty years have passed, Your Excellency, since your mother and father, the sovereign King and Queen of Nyle, ruled over a prosperous and glorious kingdom. The differences between that kingdom and the world you now know are nearly impossible to describe, but suffice it to say that the people were happy, well fed and never fearful, because the land was well protected, prosperous, and peaceful. Commerce and the arts flourished and, because of our fame and honor, courtiers, knights and noblemen from around the world called at our courts and we at theirs. The Realm of Nyle was the envy of many realms and more than equal to any other in the known world.

As you know, Sir Steven, the king and queen were seduced by a wicked witch to our great loss. The general history of what the witch did is known to you, but we have never shared the full story and the actual details of what happened at that time. Now you shall hear the tale of your twin brother, Michael, the True King of the Realm of Nyle. Although you have been spared the full story of his fate, I shall now share it with you.

You know that the king and queen were deceived into following the witch on a journey from which they never returned. However, we believe that they did not simply disappear. Instead, we believe that your parents were both murdered. We know that your brother was enchanted and trapped by the witch's magic at the same time. What's more, we believe that he may yet live. These details have been kept from you until this moment, because the events I am about to share with you took place when you were far too young to bear the sorrow of what had happened. The tragedy of what I am about to relate to you is unspeakable. Now that you are ready to hear the truth, I shall relate the full history of this sad chapter in the annals of the Maxwell family history. This tragedy placed you in the office you hold today, serving as steward over the affairs of the City of Trundle and not as our king, ruling over the Realm of Nyle.

The witch, known as Lucinda, accompanied by a black cat that was her familiar companion, arrived at the royal palace presenting herself as a gifted teacher of the children of royalty. When Lucinda came to our Realm, she was warmly welcomed into the court by your mother and father. Your parents subsequently determined that they should seek Lucinda's services in order to gain the finest education possible for their two sons.

Exercising her magic arts, Lucinda was able to deceive the king and queen, causing them to think that her wisdom knew no limits. She would change herself into a small bird, and in that form she visited the private chambers of the king and queen, hearing every word of their conversation. Thus, in time, Lucinda learned much of what your parents thought no one knew. The witch used this knowledge to play on their secret hopes and fears, manipulating them to do her bidding. The king and queen did precisely as Lucinda wished, never realizing the horrible effect that her designs would have on the kingdom and the members of the royal household.

The witch knew that if she could capture and control your brother Michael, the True King, the only remaining protection for the kingdom would be the king and queen. With those three out of the way, nothing could thwart Lucinda from realizing her dreadful ambitions. She planned to supplant the rightful rulers of the Realm of Nyle and rule in their stead.

Lucinda convinced the king and queen to permit her to take your twin brother Michael away to a special school situated in her homeland, where royal children were supposedly taught all of the wonderful arts and wisdom of her people. However, instead of sending Michael to a school for royalty, as your parents expected, Lucinda enchanted him and secretly placed him into a mirrored box that was designed to imprison him for the rest of his life. One of the walls of the magic box acted as an observation portal that allowed your brother to observe the world, and even to see you, while he remained trapped within. In summary, Sir Steven, Lucinda succeeded in placing your brother into an evil engine of everlasting bondage, an enchanted prison from which he would be powerless to escape.

Although Sir Albert and I opposed the witch publicly, and were openly skeptical of her plans, the king and queen were convinced by Lucinda that the schooling she and her people could provide to Prince Michael would make him a far better ruler. By accepting Lucinda's proposal for their son's education, the king and queen felt sure that the success of the Realm would be secured for generations to come. We were horrified to learn that your brother had been imprisoned and controlled by Lucinda. Their majesties, being convinced that their new counselor far surpassed us with our limited wisdom and skills, thought that we were merely jealous of her. Because of this false belief, which was encouraged by the witch, they allowed her to have her way with your brother Michael in spite of our protests. Sadly, the more we protested this evil course of action, the more the king and queen were convinced that they had made a wise decision in placing your brother into Lucinda's hands.

Once she had the True King under her control, Lucinda convinced the king and queen that their majesties should journey with her to learn more of her people and the special arts and knowledge of her Realm. Little did they realize that they had been seduced and, again, they refused our council. Thus, just one night after your brother had been imprisoned, the king and queen left with Lucinda, her familiar cat, and a company of mounted soldiers. The next morning we found all of our soldiers sleeping soundly. They were disoriented and dazed, because they had all been drugged. When we searched, to our dismay, both the king and queen and all of the royal gifts which they carried with them had vanished. We have never learned what happened to your parents or to the treasures. Sir Albert and I believe that once Lucinda had the king and queen in her power that she ate both of them whole, as is the custom of this kind of creature.

To conclude this history, Sir Steven, we are convinced that the witch Lucinda planned to return and take control over your brother Michael, who with the death of the king and queen is now the True King and heir of the Realm of Nyle. After Lucinda placed him inside the magic mirrored box and locked it, we never saw him again. We think that Lucinda buried the box with King Michael inside somewhere very close to the palace or under it and that she planned to return and claim her prize later after she murdered the king and queen. We believe that something unexpected happened to Lucinda which ruined her plans to take control of the Realm of Nyle. To this day, nothing has been heard of her since she left, leading your parents the king and queen to their deaths.

After hearing all that Drindle Foos has to say, the Steward bids his guests goodnight. He is deeply troubled by the news of his brother Michael. Later that night, as he dreams, he has a distressing vision. In the vision, he meets his twin brother Michael. His twin is held captive, confined inside a box lined with mirrors and hardly able to move. Michael is powerless to escape from his trap or to do anything other than passively observe the events taking place in the world outside the box. The horror of seeing his brother trapped in this closed and claustrophobic state upsets Steven so greatly that he is shaken awake from his dream, and finds himself jumping up from the bed.

Sir Steven throws on his garments and begins walking along the top of the walls of the city, pondering the meaning of the dream and the news from Drindle Foos. The Steward is perplexed as he turns the puzzle of his brother's past over in his mind. Winding his way amongst the battlements of Trundle, and through its many towers, stairs and doorways, the Steward softly speaks a greeting to each guard he passes. The guards are surprised to see their Steward pacing the walls at this hour and each wonders what troubles him. The night sky is clear, but the moon is absent from the heavens above and the darkness weighs heavily upon Steven.

Gazing into the waters of the moat surrounding the palace, Sir Steven wishes that he could know--with certainty--what really happened to his twin brother. He remembers the words of his counselors and their belief that his brother lies buried alive probably somewhere close at hand. *Perhaps Michael is alive tonight,* he thinks. *Suppose that he is lying somewhere very near where I can't see him, even under my feet?*

A nameless and faceless grief overwhelms the good Steward as he mourns the loss of his family while the night watch passes. Steven wonders why his family has suffered such a cruel and senseless fate. He is the only Maxwell remaining who can ask these questions or guess at their answers. The king and queen cannot respond to his wish for answers or his need to find meaning in this strange tragedy. The dark silence of the empty night overwhelms Steven.

Tears well up in Steven's eyes and he is unable to stop them from spilling down into the still waters of the moat below. As these tears are released from Steven's lonely, aching heart, they plummet into the darkness. As each one touches the smooth surface of the water, a faint series of circles begins to fan out on the glassy surface. Steven is alone with his tears. It is safe to cry and grieve in the darkness.

More than half an hour passes as Steven weeps quietly. The night remains dark, yet as he pauses to gaze up into the heavens above, he can see that the clouds have disappeared, and now the sky is filled with the bright and glorious stars of early spring. Each star is a unique and shining jewel. The stars evoke memories of his family, his mother's bright eyes, Michael's smiles, and the warm presence of his father.

Steven wipes his eyes dry and prepares to return to his quarters in hopes that he can stop thinking of his brother and family long enough to get some sleep. As his eyes clear, he stares carefully, thirty feet below, at a point on the surface of the water. Off slightly to his left, there is a faint glow of light coming from a source that seems to lie below the smooth surface of the water. Steven moves closer, to check what he is seeing, looking directly down at the light. *Is this a mirage, perhaps a reflection from the lights of the City, or is it a phantom of the vision of his brother that has remained stuck in his mind?* No, the glow is faint, but it *is* coming from the water in the moat. The source of light must be underneath the water, not above!

Forgetting his grief, Sir Steven tears off his outer coat and dives headlong into the waters below, seeking to reach the source of the light. Guards stationed nearby hear the loud splash of a heavy object. Suspecting foul play, they sound the alarm and all of them rush together with torches lifted high to see what has happened. They can see that the waters of the moat have been disturbed, but none guess that it is their own steward who has broken the spell of the night.

Down in the depths of the moat, swimming hard in the dark water, Steven can see the source of the light more clearly. The soft glow is coming through a smooth, glass surface on the bottom! Steven can dimly make out what looks like a figure on the other side of the glass. Steven reaches out with his right hand and touches the smooth and unyielding surface. However, when he reaches with his left hand, both his hand and forearm pass right through the glass, penetrating inside and into the interior of what is on the other side of the glassy surface. Strangely, while his body is immersed in the cold water and his right hand rests on the hard surface of glass, his left hand and forearm have passed through and he can sense a dry space and warm air inside. Steven gasps with surprise and, needing air, instinctively pushes up toward the surface above. Just as he begins to push, a hand from within the box grasps his left hand tightly and in that moment, not one, but two men rise to the surface.

Both Steven and the man from below are gasping for air and in a state of shock. Sir Steven calls for help and the guards who are standing nearby, dumbfounded, hold their torches forward trying to understand what is taking place. They rush to Sir Steven's aid. Then Sir Steven catches his breath and gasping loudly says to the stranger, *Are you Michael? Are you my beloved brother Michael?*

The man from below tries to speak, but can only smile. At last, he finds his voice and he manages to blurt out. *Yes, I am your twin brother Michael! Thank God you have finally discovered me for you have set me free from Lucinda's enchanted trap!*

Before the sun has risen, the wonderful news that Steven's long-lost brother has been discovered spreads quickly through the city and beyond the city walls. Everyone is excitedly talking about the fact that Michael, the True King has been found alive and well!

After talking the situation over with King Michael and forming a plan of action, Sir Steven and his counselors agree to publish the news of the True King's return with a formal proclamation that will be posted in the city square. The history of the True King may then be read and understood by all the citizens of Trundle. King Michael expresses a wish to give his greetings to the good citizens of Trundle in a separate proclamation written in his own hand, which he finishes that very night.

King Michael lays out his plan for the future. He wishes to set out immediately for his royal palace in order that his reign as True King should be restored without delay. He informs Sir Steven and his counselors that his throne belongs next to the ocean, not in City of Trundle. The grounds of the royal palace actually overlook the sea, on the easternmost limits of the Realm of Nyle. He invites Sir Steven, Sir Albert and Bishop Henry Farsight, to join him accompanied by twelve guards on a journey to the abandoned royal palace.

King Michael explains to Steven that, in spite of his long absence, much work had been done to complete the foundations and structures of his palace before Lucinda stopped the work by imprisoning him within her magic box. Michael notes that those foundations should still be intact and that the original designs for the palace will reveal themselves again and guide them in their future work of restoration. He then informs his companions that a wonderful thing is about to happen: *The Kingdom of Nyle will be resurrected shortly, and when it is, we shall again see its true splendor!* But before the work can begin, King Michael tells them, he must be present at his palace where he will reign as the True King.

At noon of the next day, the entourage of the King sets out. The four noblemen are accompanied by twelve mounted guards followed by a cart and driver pulled by a pair of donkeys. The cart carries the King's tent, throne, writing desk and the group's supplies. Hopeful cheers are offered by the townspeople as the travelers depart from the city, two by two. In their thoughts, the king's companions are gripped by uncertainty, not sure if they should hope for better days ahead, not sure if it is wise to believe that Michael is the True King of the Realm of Nyle.

As they journey, King Michael and Sir Steven ride side by side, sharing their thoughts and looking more and more like twins as the hours pass. Those who watched the brothers as they rode out of the city noted a regal bearing about Michael, a manner of handling his horse, his way of looking, speaking and listening that is not so apparent in Steven. They look alike outwardly, but there are subtle differences in their manner, countenance and bearing. Those differences are plainly visible in close proximity to the True King. As the travelers draw nearer and nearer to the True King's palace, each can sense the embers of newborn hope in their hearts beginning to kindle deep within.

As they ride together, Sir Steven retells the sad history of the Maxwell family, filling King Michael in on the details of their past. The King is deeply grieved by this history and saddened that so much time has passed while he was locked away and unable to govern the affairs of the Realm. The news that the ships of True no longer call at the ports of Nyle shocks the King, but even more upsetting is the fact that it is no longer safe for the citizens of the realm to travel and trade in safety. The powerful demeanor of the travelers must have been evident to those who watched them from afar for the group arrives without interruption at the grounds where King Michael has said that his royal palace is located. As the sun sets, the King's tent is pitched and, before twilight has faded away, dinner is roasted and eaten with pleasure. The members of the party then eagerly turn in for a much needed nights rest, while the guards on duty take their posts for the first watch of the night.

Steven is impressed with his brother. He notes that Michael makes almost no effort to be in charge, yet he is the natural master of events. There is an inexplicable but inherent majesty in everything that he says and does. His vision of the future is deep, while his thoughts and movements flow together naturally, each one following smoothly after the other. Every man in the group is completely at ease with their newly emerged King.

Knowing the dismal state of the Realm, as well as his own frustration and inability to change its destiny, Steven knows full well that he could never fulfill the Kingdom's need for the gifts inherent in the True King. A growing understanding is developing within Steven and those with him that King Michael has the gifts that are needed to rule well and to be a blessing to his subjects. An inexplicable richness and power seems to reside within Michael. The growing awareness of Michael's sovereign nature makes every member of the entourage glad to be with the True King and supporting his reign.

In the first light of dawn everyone wakes and stands huddled together in the soft breeze of early morning to quietly watch the golden sun rising smoothly up over the distant horizon of the sea. As the sun travels upward, they turn their backs to its brightness and face the surrounding terrain to get a good look at the palace grounds in the early morning light. The party searches to discern the lines of the various structures while their backs are warmed by the golden sunshine.

In that moment, King Michael directs everyone's attention to a large raised structure situated directly in front of the group that stands out clearly in the morning light. Rising more than ten feet above the ground they are standing on is a platform large enough for hundreds of people to stand on. Once they reach the structure and clamber up to the top, they find a remarkable sight. From this vantage point, they can gaze west, looking back into the Realm from which they have journeyed. Far below and behind them, the ocean waves can be seen breaking on sandy beaches to the east. To the north and the south, the land stretches for many miles before it fades out of sight. Those standing on the platform are startled to realize that from this vantage point, they have an unobstructed view on any point on the compass that extends to a distance of more than thirty miles.

King Michael bids his men to lose no time as they work together to clear the debris from the platform area. Soon they find that what seemed to be a flat, debris-covered surface is really a polished marble floor lying hidden beneath their feet. Sir Albert is stunned. With new eyes he scans the area being cleared and he begins to see, and then recognize numerous designs and details that exist in the floor. Seen as a whole, the area that they are working on must be the floor of a throne room without a roof! The design, quality and precision of the abandoned structure mark it as the product of master planners and craftsmen. Sir Albert shakes his head in wonder, recognizing what is evidently an undertaking of great craft and magnitude, yet one of which he had been completely ignorant.

The floor is roughly fifty paces wide by one hundred paces long. Working quickly, with their curiosity to spur them on, it takes the group a full day to remove the accumulated debris from the floor, and to restore something of the glassy finish of the polished marble surface. Both the King and Sir Steven are enchanted by the inlaid patterns of colored marble and the precise complexity of the inlaid artwork. There are many designs and symbols, skillfully worked into the shining surface, which are now fully legible.

King Michael explains that they are in fact standing in the throne room of his palace and that the symbols they can now see worked into a large circle form the markings of an instrument, which are in fact the points of a large compass. Sir Albert, who is too old to continue the hard work of polishing the floor, takes a moment to stand back from the work and get a bigger perspective on the picture that has been revealed in the artwork. Because he is resting, he is the first to see the puzzle that lies hidden within the pattern of the compass.

Why, these compass points are reversed! Our east is its west, our west is its east; everything has been shifted, mirror reversed! Remembering that King Michael had been trapped in a mirrored box, Sir Albert adds, *King Michael, might the strange shift indicated in this compass device here in your throne room have something to do with what Lucinda did to you, something connected to the enchantments she used to trap you in her magic box?* King Michael is unable to answer his counselor, but asks that everyone remain working until the cleanup has been finished.

Once the work of clearing and polishing is done, the King gathers his full entourage together and asks Bishop Henry Farsight to lead the group in a prayer of thanks. Starting with the Bishop, each member asks for God's mercy upon the True King, on the Realm, and on the work of restoration that is now underway. Many a tear is shed to the sounds of *Amen!* as the heart of each one is poured out, sharing inner thoughts and hopes that the Realm would once again be blessed. Bishop Farsight invokes the Lord's blessings on the True King and his people. He invokes the Lord's wisdom, power and mercy upon the King and upon all those he will serve as he rules under God's authority. The Bishop closes by asking that God grant the True King His grace and His ability to express the designs that are resident within him, ready to be engaged in service and rich blessing to his people.

The True King's first task involves composing messages and dispatching them to the Lords of the Realm, to its workers, and to its artisans and many others who must be summoned at once to join him at the palace. The True King wishes to marshal an organization of talented men and women at once to carry out the mission of restoring the kingdom. As directed by the king, the throne and writing desk are unpacked and placed precisely on the platform in the center of the compass motif. Michael warms up to the long task ahead with a series of writing exercises and then he begins to write his summons. As he works, Michael dips his feather quill that is cut for use by a left-handed writer. He dips the quill into a bottle of ink before writing out each passage of the messages in a smooth and flowing hand. In rapid order, each of twelve administrative messages are composed and sealed in packets for delivery.

As soon as the King finishes writing the first twelve messages, the twelve mounted couriers who are to deliver them arrive. Each one has been called to appear for this purpose by an unspoken summons. All twelve riders dismount and appear before the King, ready to do his bidding. It seems as if each rider is dreaming, yet wide-eyed and filled with purpose. Each courier is given instructions for his journey and then given his letter and final encouragement by the King, who urges them to make haste. One by one the messengers gallop off to deliver the King's messages to different points of the compass.

Next, another twelve mounted couriers arrive in like manner and each in turn is given a diplomatic update to convey to the rulers of the lands surrounding the Realm of Nyle. This second party of mounted couriers has also been summoned by the True King's unspoken wish. When the errand of the second group of riders is completed, all those who live in neighboring realms shall know that Michael, the True King of Nyle, has been restored to his throne.

On an intuitive level, Michael knows what is needed, what must be written and done, and how to do it in the most efficient manner. The King's messages inevitably elicit a willing response and all who are summoned respond without delay. Soon, the courier corps alone numbers more than 1,000 mounts and riders. By the King's wish, couriers are stationed at strategic points throughout the Realm. In a matter of days, news spreads to all that the True King is present in his palace and in charge of the affairs of the Realm. King Michael is given the full support and allegiance of his subjects. The understanding that the kingdom has been given new life warms the hearts of all who are touched by the affairs of the Realm.

As the first day of King Michael's reign at the royal palace comes to an end, the sun drops down behind the mountains on the Western limits of the Realm. The sky over the kingdom is filled with feathery pink clouds that turn to deep purple as the night approaches. Everyone in the King's entourage is exhausted. After a hearty meal, the only members of the group who remain awake are the four guards who are posted on the outskirts of the camp.

The guards notice that the night sky has turned a very dark black. It is so black that the stars are no longer visible. This strange darkness hovers over the face of the land until the ground beneath them begins to tremble, as if in agony. Everyone in the King's entourage is aroused from their sound sleep and jolted into a state of disorientation and panic. The wild shaking leaves everyone reeling in disequilibrium, unable to understand what is happening until the shaking subsides and the stars return. At dawn, the most amazing thing happens: the sun begins to rise precisely where it had set over the mountains the night before. Instead of rising from the sea, the sun is rising above the mountains, over the Realm of Nyle!

In the welcome light of dawn, everyone can see what has taken place with their own eyes. The world itself has somehow been reversed, as if some kind of a magic mirror that held it fast had been shattered during the night. In the long hours of darkness and shaking, something incredible has taken place: west has been made into east, and east into west. The globe, with all of its oceans and lands has been turned around, like a toy top that is now spinning in the opposite direction from that in which it was spinning the night before!

The Realm of Nyle is now aligned perfectly with the points of the compass pattern inlaid on the marble floor of the True King's throne room. The hidden wisdom of the king's decision to return immediately to his palace grounds, and his purpose for doing so, are now fully apparent. Everyone in the True King's company is struck silent by the manner in which the surface of the floor perfectly illustrates the precise details and structure of a world that has just been reborn. The effort that was put into cleaning the King's throne room has exposed the key they needed to understand the puzzle of the prior night.

Over the next several days and weeks, the work of King Michael begins in earnest as his subjects clear the roads, open up the harbors of the Realm and prepare to welcome the first wave of merchants and diplomats coming to visit the realm from far-off lands. Talented men and women who had fled the sadness of Nyle return to assist in meeting its diplomatic needs, and to serve in key administrative, artistic, military, and commercial posts. One of the most notable changes which occurs as a result of the True King's return to power is the end of the sad and tedious demeanor of the realm. In comparison to the drab garments worn before, rich and vibrant-- colored clothing is now worn by the people and this too lifts spirits.

The bright spirit and fresh life that everyone feels is expressed in every setting. Ceremonies of all kinds begin springing up spontaneously. New experiences melt away the sadness of the past and bring a warm energy which courses through the hearts of everyone in the Kingdom. Because so much that was impossible before is now possible, the older citizens of Nyle are almost in a state of shock, running about with their mouths agape, reveling in their unexpected good fortune. The deep wonder of what has actually happened inspires many hearts and minds.

With the healing of the realm well underway, the True King and Sir Steven decide that the time has finally come to return to the City of Trundle. As they approach the city, Sir Steven's eyes are filled with tears of joy as he and his brother are greeted with admiration, wonder, and words of love. Those who once could barely survive have prepared a lavish feast to celebrate the return of Sir Steven and the True King. There will be dancing and entertainments, toasts and speeches, and a rich, plentiful banquet open to all. A fireworks show will be staged over the waters of the palace moat after the sun sets. Like all of the other subjects in the Realm, the citizens of Trundle are filled with an abiding joy and awestruck wonder at the new lives they are now living and are looking forward to celebrating with the king.

The miraculous changes Sir Steven saw while he was at the king's palace overlooking the ocean, had all been wrought within the context of the unfamiliar. But since returning to the familiar setting of the City of Trundle after an absence of many months, Sir Steven can hardly believe his eyes; for plainly, the city and its people are completely transformed, almost to the point of being unrecognizable.

No! These are *my people and this* is *my city--the home of those who once lived in fear and misery, who were dragged down by the burden of their lives and barely able to survive. Yes! I recognize the city. It is the place where we once lived in sorrow, but now Trundle is filled with joy, music, singing, merriment, and ceremonies. Now, our own merchants are planning to travel to other cities and far off realms. The fields are being farmed with the blessings of good weather and our abundant crops will soon be harvested and stored for export. I see high-quality imported goods everywhere, while our merchants are busy producing goods of their own that we can sell in return. And best of all, the forces of cold, darkness, perplexity and hopelessness, that once strangled and smothered us, have melted away, evaporated!*

The happy pleasure of seeing his town and people so energized, safe, and free to live joyfully, is overwhelming to Steven. Since his inner experience is beyond words, tears must suffice.

That night, the citizens of Trundle gather to feast and meet their King, to raise toasts of honor and thanks for the blessed night when he was rescued from the confines of his prison beneath the castle moat by his loyal twin brother. After the preliminary speeches of the nobles and administrators, the True King rises to speak to his people. His words warm the heart of all who hear them.

Finally, the True King and his Co-Regent Steven join in with all of the citizens of the Realm of Nyle for a magnificent fireworks show. The dazzling display of art, which has been imported for the occasion, is supervised by Drindle Foos, who besides being the court historian was also very fond of fireworks.

Oh, by the way, early the following Spring, King Michael marries Princess Caravelle, daughter of King Chauntly of the Realm of True. But that's another story.

The end.

FROM FABLE TO FACT ~ CHAPTER 6

A man must know his destiny . . . if he does not recognize it, then he is lost. By this I mean, once, twice, or at the very most, three times, fate will reach out and tap a man on the shoulder . . . if he has the imagination, he will turn around and fate will point out to him what fork in the road he should take, if he has the guts, he will take it.

General George S. Patton

One of the advantages of telling stories is the way a story can bring us into a new imaginative world that reflects some hidden truths about our own world. When I first began to write with my left hand, I did not realize that, like the True King in the fable, I would be initiating a cascade of developments that had been frozen in the limbo of a submergee spell for nearly four decades. When I placed the first stroke of the pen onto paper with the knowledge that it was the *real me* doing the writing, it was like awakening after an unnaturally long sleep. Knowing that I could restore what had been lost, and acting on that knowledge, was like putting a key into a lock and turning it to open a closed door.

There were literally hundreds of personal surprises in waiting for me as the details of my new self began to surface.

The following image shows the first sentence I wrote with the clear understanding that I was writing it as a naturally left-handed person (see Figure 7).

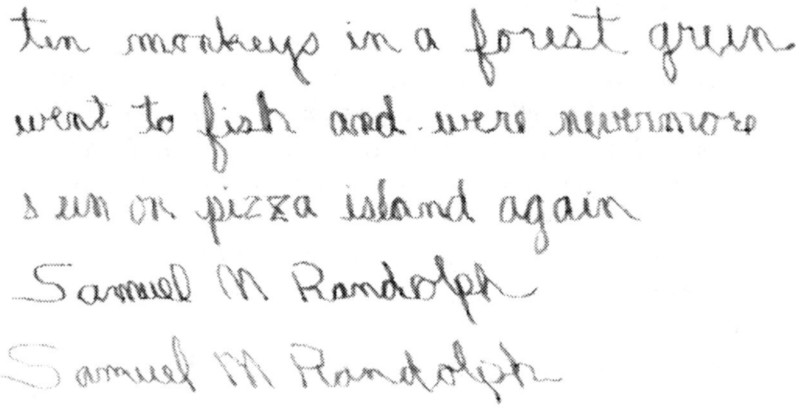

ten monkeys in a forest green
went to fish and were nevermore
s un on pizza island again
Samuel M Randolph
Samuel M Randolph

Figure 7.

The process of becoming an emergee began with a few simple decisions that set the course for the long journey I was setting out on:

Decision one: *Because I had positive verification from my parents that I was, in fact, born left-handed, I decided that my signature should be the product of my left-hand. Henceforth, I would sign all checks and legal documents with my left hand.*

Decision two: *If I was born left-handed, then a primary marker of that fact was handwriting. The fact that the pathway to submerge function was strongly associated with writing meant that reversing course made perfectly good sense if I wished to emerge. On that basis, I decided that henceforth, all of my writing would be performed using my left hand.*

Decision three: *Insofar as possible, all skilled functions including sports that required fine coordination, eating with*

51

utensils, brushing teeth, opening doors, drawing pictures and any other skilled use of the hands that had once been performed with my right hand, would be transferred over and completed using my left hand.

Decision four: *To celebrate these changes and to confirm my new identity, I felt that I needed a name that harmonized with my new identity. I chose to be called solely by my legal name-- Samuel-- and dropped the use of its truncated form, Sam.*

During the first several months following my discovery, I regularly felt like a butterfly shedding its cocoon and emerging to find a new body with wings. A cascade of *Ah ha!* moments came upon me as I became caught up in a current of change which initiated a series of adjustments to my left-handedness that I hadn't expected to encounter.

I had somehow managed to trigger a sequence of events that were quickly re-inventing me. All of this came as an exhilarating surprise. Each change and insight was linked to a moment of wonder, the kind we expect to see in children, but not in adults. A deeper and more finely detailed sensory awareness was building each day. Formerly frozen parts of me were thawing out and beginning to open up in me, enabling smoother, faster and more accurate movement of hand and body. With so many powerful changes taking place in this quickly moving stream of new experiences, the first months of discovery swept me off my feet, and in many ways I became a child again. I was pleasantly enchanted and even comfortable with these developments, so instead of panicking, I chose to continue on with the adventure in spite of the fact that I knew I was being changed forever.

Illustrating what happened during the first few months after emerging as a left-hander has proven to be a difficult task. Many of the changes happened so fast that they didn't even register in my mind at the time. The start of the emergee process might be compared to the initial rush that a person in a kayak feels when they first commit themselves to powerful forces that exist in the rapids of a large flowing river. I was piloting a metaphorical kayak into the rapids of change by choosing to emerge and the forces of growth and development that had been held in check for a lifetime were now hard at work in my body and mind. As these currents were released, I was carried along briskly by the unleashed forces of change.

Because my body and mind were finally being allowed to work as originally intended, the forces of change seemed to run as if they were directed by a hidden master guidance system. The autopilot directed developmental changes in my body and mind so they would take place in an orderly and efficient sequence. In hindsight, I can see that I was experiencing an accelerated version of the same process in that we all undergo as we mature into adulthood in concert with our own plan for growth, our *genetic blueprint*.

Once the floodgates in the dam that had been holding me back were opened, the pent up life energy within was free from the unhappy constraints of the past. Like a chick that had finally broken out of its eggshell, the growth and development that were to follow would occur as a natural consequence. The design and forces of life that were to be expressed and enjoyed were unleashed. I had been set free.

The long years of frustration and the sense of being bottled up inside were coming to an end. Since writing was the key behavior I had learned to reverse in order to become a submergee, I reasoned that left-handed writing was the first behavior I needed to express in order to recover from the training. Like a young child going to school, I began to write in a left-handed cursive form for an hour or more each day.

Using computers as an analogy for what happens when an emergee process is initiated, consider the "housekeeping" or maintenance programs that we use to keep our computers running efficiently. As these programs run, an observer who is only aware of messages being sent to the computer screen would tend to think that the program is really performing a simple task. In fact, whole files can be deleted or moved, drives and devices optimized, virus scans and quarantines run, and specialized repairs can be made in addition to large-scale system updates. All of these intensive--and sometimes complex--tasks are normally completed off-screen or, as they were in my case, automatically and unconsciously. In the same way that computer maintenance programs work to enhance processing efficiency at a global level, the neurological updates and developments that served to optimize the diverse pieces of my body and mind worked together to optimize the function of my biological system.

Contrary to intuition, the biological version of what has been described above is, in fact, far more complex than it seems to be. Upon close inspection, the interrelated systems that must work together to make life possible are actually based upon exquisitely detailed mechanisms and very precisely coordinated events. Then, there are higher-order mysteries to unravel, such as the finely tuned design, function, and integration of our complex sensory systems. And, there are other puzzles that we may never solve such as the question of how biological systems support consciousness and memory.

As we look at them with deeper and more complete understanding, we realize that all of these living systems are actually more, not less detailed than we would naturally think they were. In terms of what we know today about living systems, our confident parallels between computers and living systems can now look comically forced.

The notion that something as complex as a shift from submergee to emergee status is possible, that a change which entails wholesale alterations of physical functions and neurological organization can take place, becomes much easier to accept in light of our developing insights into biological systems. The marvelous plasticity and organization that biological entities demonstrate in maintaining life processes, and in responding to internal and external pressures, sets the stage for the dramatic events of an emergee experience. Give a submergee the appropriate opportunity to initiate emergee behaviors that restart a preprogrammed biological repertoire, and combine this behavior with conscious intention, and what do you get? Voila! The submergee human's system can optimize itself. If this level of change proves normative on a large scale for other humans as it did for me, the flexibility demonstrated by humans (biological entities) who emerge in this manner would be impressive.

A rather dramatic story that supports the emergee theme is told by the famous neurologist Oliver Sacks, M.D., who writes about a patient he refers to as *Miss J* in an article titled *Hands*.[6] The blind patient that Sacks portrays described her hands as "Useless Godforsaken lumps of dough - they don't even feel part of me." This patient was sixty years old when Sacks first encountered her. She had to be fed by others because of her "useless" hands. In time, Sacks discovered that there was nothing organically wrong with Miss J's hands. For her entire life she had believed, incorrectly, that they were nothing more than useless appendages.

The key that unlocked this "emergee experience of the hands" for Sack's patient was the unexpected knowledge that it was possible for her to use them. Miss J's "emergee process" began with a linkage of mind and movement that took place with the first voluntary use of her hands (Sacks describes her becoming hungry and impatient enough to reach out and grasp a bagel). Miss J's first volitional act began a wondrous synthesis of development and discovery that ultimately completed her intact, but heretofore incomplete developmental process. She began to deliberately use her hands for the first time. Like a dormant garden that had been lifeless for sixty years, Miss J's two limp hands sprang back to life and began to bloom with regular use.

By learning to actively use her hands, Miss J entered into a new world of tactile experiences that she had never known before. She simply needed to begin using both hands rather than remaining passive as if she had the hands of a zombie. In my case, I needed to become left-handed in order to initiate a similar process, one that affected the manner in which I related not only to my hands, but to my entire being. As a submergee, I believed I was something I was not. Until the perceptual and functional advances I began to experience as an emergee taught me that I was someone else, someone who didn't have the old limits to hold him back, I had no way of seeing the invisible doors and walls of the submergee prison I was living in.

ILLUSTRATING AN EMERGEE JOURNEY

The journey of a kayaker paddling down-river provides an excellent illustration of the sensory experiences of an emergee. A river journey of this kind captures something of the pairing of volitional choice (paddling) and automatic process (riding the river) that occurred with me.

On a sensory level, I was like a kayaker who is supported by a large body of water--water that has been set free from a dam that once constrained it. The body of moving water was free to move energetically because I chose to remove the constraining forces by deciding to make the emergee journey. The driving force of that water worked like a flood of unleashed forces--forces that had a job to do. The accelerated development of skills that came in this flood of change included processing enhancements and improved tactile, kinetic, visual, and auditory abilities, to name a few. The persistent flooding of the senses that I experienced as this took place was something that a kayaker might describe as the rush of taking a thrilling ride through a very powerful set of rapids.

On a cognitive level, my mind had to learn to navigate through the newly enhanced environments that were created by the emergee process. Changes in my thought process took place as a consequence of the improved sensory, memory and mental resources that I enjoyed. In functional terms, I sensed that I was operating in a shifting setting, one that liberated and enhanced cognitive processing. As time passed, I developed enhanced skills and was able to function and move through life much more efficiently.

THE TOOLS OF THE TRADE ~ WRITING THERAPY

To become left-handed, I reasoned that I needed to retrace the steps I had originally taken in becoming right-handed. The most obvious area for submergee training was handwriting exercises. So with confidence that copying drills done in cursive form with my left hand would be the perfect therapy for me, I went to work.

For paper, I used lined yellow legal size pads and a smooth flowing roller ball pen. I found that my choice of pen for these exercises was very important because even a small amount of resistance in the pen made the learning process less effective. For a source to copy from, I chose the Bible as an inspiring and grammatically accurate reference book. This source had the added advantage of incorporating chapter and verse references, which added structure and reference points and because both numbers and letters were being copied.

I began my copying work knowing only that it felt like the right thing to do. As I moved the pen along the paper, I felt as if I was being guided on my way by the lines on the paper. I often saw them as twin railings, one on each side of a steep set of stairs. I dated each session, and copied all of the numbered verse references as I worked. A host of new insights always came to me while I was copying so that every session was rewarding in a different way. Each time I finished my work, I realized that I had improved my writing skills and that in addition, many other equally important tasks that had to do with to processing the details of the emergee experience were also being addressed.

As these first several days passed in the copying exercises, both my mind and body were challenged by the speed, quantity and power of the changes that flowed from the work. As noted earlier, the system of my body and mind seemed to be running some sort of a powerful housekeeping program that was busy doing the work it needed to do to support the emergee process. If I were to assign a name for the program that made this happen, I would call it the *end-of-exile program* or perhaps the *restoration-of-what-was-meant-to-be program*. This program had apparently been initiated at the moment that I understood for the first time that I was left-handed and then chose to shift my identity and behavior accordingly. As the new systems developed, I sensed that I was leaving parts of my old self behind and in the process, becoming a new person.

At some points in my journey I recognized that as many as three significant developments directly related to the emergee growth process had taken place in a single day. At other times, changes such as these occurred only once or twice a week. Although it wasn't apparent at the time, these changes required integration within the systems of my body and mind and that part of the developmental process took time. An example that comes to mind was the alteration of memory processing. As an emergee, I can now recall memories with clear visual images. While this visual memory was developing, I could sense that my memory system was a work-in-process for a period of several weeks. Once that process had been completed, I developed a very useful visual memory that enabled me to recall objects I had seen. My memory process had been upgraded, but a time of integration was required before those improved resources became available to me.

Every few days, I would take a moment to pause and "pull my kayak out of the river" to lie quietly for a few hours, and reflect on my emergee journey. In those relaxing interludes, it became apparent to me that some very long distances had been covered. One day I was pleased to discover that I had developed a much finer sense of coordination and faster reflexes. I recalled the moment I was first able to catch a fly in mid-air with my left hand. The increase in speed and coordination I now had as an emergee was such that my reaction speed enabled me to reach out and catch a falling glass rather that watch helplessly as I had in the past. My new-found athletic ability continues to be a real source of pleasure every time I get a chance to test it, because these skills were notably absent the entire time I lived as a submergee.

I discovered that I could now toss a crumpled piece of paper--or any other small object into a wastebasket, having complete confidence that I would hit my target. I was able to catch with ease any object that was thrown to me. I also realized that when my hands contacted these objects, that I was catching them much more comfortably and tightly than before, and that the catching process required far less concentration. These *Yippee-how about that!* moments were mixed in with many others that were similar in nature, all testifying to me that things were changing in a dramatic manner, that I was continuing to change in significant and unexpected ways. As I reflected on these discoveries, I realized that my emergee journey of many seemingly uneventful days had in fact resulted in changes that I could never have imagined. I gradually began to get a clear understanding of the depth and scale of what was taking place.

The picture of a river journey serves as a good illustration for my travels, since it provides a linear framework that can be used to bring together the many interconnected and layered changes that occurred with the passage of time. Once I had entered into the current of left-handedness with a few dedicated strokes of the paddle (my roller ball pen) the river system (my body and mind) affirmed the wisdom of my choice to head downstream, and off I went. Had I looked back, I would have noticed that the gates of the dam, now far upstream, were opening up wider and wider, as each day passed. This fortuitous release of life energy brought my developmental river up to the flood stage as the habits and beliefs that had imprisoned me for forty years were abandoned.

I sensed that I had become someone else, someone other than Sam. There truly was a new self emerging from within me. I grew to understand that I was a more talented and gifted person than I thought I was, someone whom I now refer to as Samuel. As I began to see my life history more clearly from the new perspectives that had formed within me, I understood that I had been tricked into damming up the preferences and habits that were placed within, preferences that now served to guide and empower me on my journey to becoming Samuel. The dammed up submergee version of self I developed as a child, whom I now refer to as Sam, was an altered version of the real me, a mere shadow of what I was intended to be. The further down river I went, the better I became acquainted with Samuel.

Samuel M. Randolph

RIDING THE DEVELOPMENTAL ELEVATOR

The paths I followed in my emergee recovery appear to have significant parallels to those that guide the developmental process that takes place in a normal human growth cycle from birth to adulthood. The difference between my emergee experience and the normal and much slower process is that parts of my journey were interrupted, or put on hold for forty years. The difference between one experience and the other is that the sequence of developments remain uninterrupted in a normal growth cycle, whereas the submergee child's growth process is altered. It appears as if in some sense, this alteration puts portions of the human developmental program into a holding mode.

As soon as my emergee travels began, I would say that those elements of my developmental process which had been halted were restarted. I found myself moving rapidly through a series of perceptual shifts that seemed to parallel the patterns of a resurrected growth sequence. If the normal growth process could be compared to climbing a ladder one rung at a time, the emergee version of that same experience would be like traveling on an elevator. Because of its slow pace, the normal growth process is effectively imperceptible on a day-to-day basis. In contrast, my process took place so quickly that it left a series of very memorable impressions behind.

One of the biggest perceptual surprises of my emergee experience was a major change in the way my visual system functioned. To use a word-image to describe what happened visually, it was as if my eyes had been merely sipping in the light through two narrow drinking straws. After emerging, the straws seemed to have grown into fire hoses--virtually flooding my mind with visual input. This difference became particularly noticeable when I was outdoors observing the fall colors.

Having access to this larger stream of information had many consequences. For example, a few weeks after I began my handwriting copy work, I realized that I could first scan the phrase I would be copying and then visualize and capture an entire block of words in my mind's eye before I began to copy the words onto the page. This was an enchanting discovery because this same talent for forming letters, words, and whole sentences in my mind could be used to sculpt letters in the air. Once I realized I could form letters by tracing them in the air with my fingers, I began to write whole words and then sentences, as if they were floating and suspended in space. This *air writing* was a skill that I had never known before. It was great fun to find out that I could use my visual system for this kind of artistic exploration and expression.

I began to *attack,* to aggressively memorize longer and longer written phrases. I learned that I could read whole sentences and then copy them, working purely from memory. The addition of these new talents alone would have been a significant boost to my collection of life skills, but I realized that they were only small parts of a much larger puzzle that was being assembled. As the pieces of the puzzle were gradually falling into place, I found them forming a new picture that was adding up to a transformed me--a new sense of self.

As my writing skills improved, I found a great deal of joy in the artistic aspects of writing. Simple devices like a flourish at the end of a word or experimenting with the loops, dots and other features of letters allowed me to play a bit, to cut loose while working in the new environment of cursive expression. Something as simple as crossing the top of the letter *t* or a series of letter *t*'s with a confident sense of style and a longer than usual crossing line brought with it a real sense of accomplishment and pride. The same aesthetic happiness was also present in dotting the letter *i,* placing a period at the end of the sentence, or even writing out a number or letter and noting that left-handed letters are formed in reverse order by the pen in some cases, such as the letter *O* or the numeral zero. On a larger scale, seeing graphic evidence that I was producing uniform, left-leaning slants with neat, even spacing between letters and words was like living in a dream. The very process that had once produced a deeply-felt embarrassment now lifted me up and gave me joy, providing an endless stream of hard evidence that I had made the right choice.

Six weeks after I began my writing exercises, to my amazement I discovered that I no longer needed lined paper for the copying process. I had learned a new skill and was able to write many successive lines of accurate horizontal script on blank sheets of paper! Equally surprising was the revelation that I could do this without any real effort. With the incremental addition of each new skill, my eyes were opened wider to the reality that a new *me* was emerging. A particularly important insight occurred, as I developed neat and flowing writing skills that were the product of someone who had mature visual skills, someone who routinely produced a neat and flowing cursive script. This evidence was especially influential to me because it provided me with undeniable evidence of skills which had been suppressed, and I was confronted with that evidence on a daily basis, thanks to my copying work.

The fact that I now possessed excellent writing skills--skills that could only have surfaced as a consequence of hidden talent--was impossible to ignore. As the evidence poured forth onto the yellow tablets, I could see that I was rounding an important corner. My new handwriting acted like a compass, telling me without a doubt that I was headed in the right direction.

Hours passed as I completed my writing exercises, and each moment of observation and contemplation brought fresh insight. The exercises gave me time to develop a better sense of who I was, what was taking place in my life, and what I was leaving behind. A slow conversation relative to my true identity was taking place, as I saw the work of a skilled and even an artistic person flowing onto each page. The expression of skill and artistic joy grew deeper as one writing exercise followed another. The history of my old submergee habits and my assumptions about who I was and what I was capable of was left further behind with each copying session.

Writing therapy helped in several important areas. It provided me with a means of focusing my mind on the process of learning new skills. While I was learning, I found that the discipline of writing sharpened my awareness of the many changes that were taking place concurrent with the improvement in my writing skills. For example, memories of my past, which I was actively considering at this time, came forth. The memories appeared in an enhanced manner and it was almost as if they were seen under a microscope or on a brightly lit stage. This allowed me to compare present experiences, which were already intensified by the rush of sensory enhancements, with those of the past. As I invested time in the copying work, I entered into a state of mind that could be classified as both therapeutic and entertaining. The sessions also helped bolster my internal sense of confidence that *all was well with my world* as I took on the daunting challenge of using my new left-handed writing skills at work.

AN EMERGEE GOES TO WORK

Switching handwriting at work was a major challenge because I use the phone extensively and have to take notes quickly. There were many times when I wondered if my juvenile looking left-handed writing would be legible to those with whom I worked because of the time pressures we routinely work under. As it turned out, my new handwriting skills stood up to the time-stress test. The writing therapy sessions helped me gain the confidence I needed to remain aware of the writing experience as it took place and to write quickly and neatly enough for my own use and also for others who might have to read my notes later. I continued my copying exercises after each workday. Retaining that discipline was vitally important as it helped me to *re-set* my writing to non-hurried standards and to keep my physiological, mental, and emotional bearings grounded as I reflected on the events of the day.

The need to make my emergee transition viable at work placed added pressures on me that the copying exercises helped channel and control. Similar to the practice of immersing a student into a new language by placing them in an environment in which that language is spoken exclusively, I was immersed in the process of using of my new writing skills. The practice sessions helped to add support to the learning process and to shorten the learning curve. I soon found that the handwriting I produced at work was not only legible, but much improved over my old right-handed printing.

As you can see from this early sample of writing from a copy exercise completed two weeks after I began my emergee process, there was much to learn (see figure 8). I had to begin at a fairly awkward level of written expression and then transfer this skill into the work environment (see figure 9). Contrast these early samples of writing with a current sample taken from a copy exercise (see figure 10).

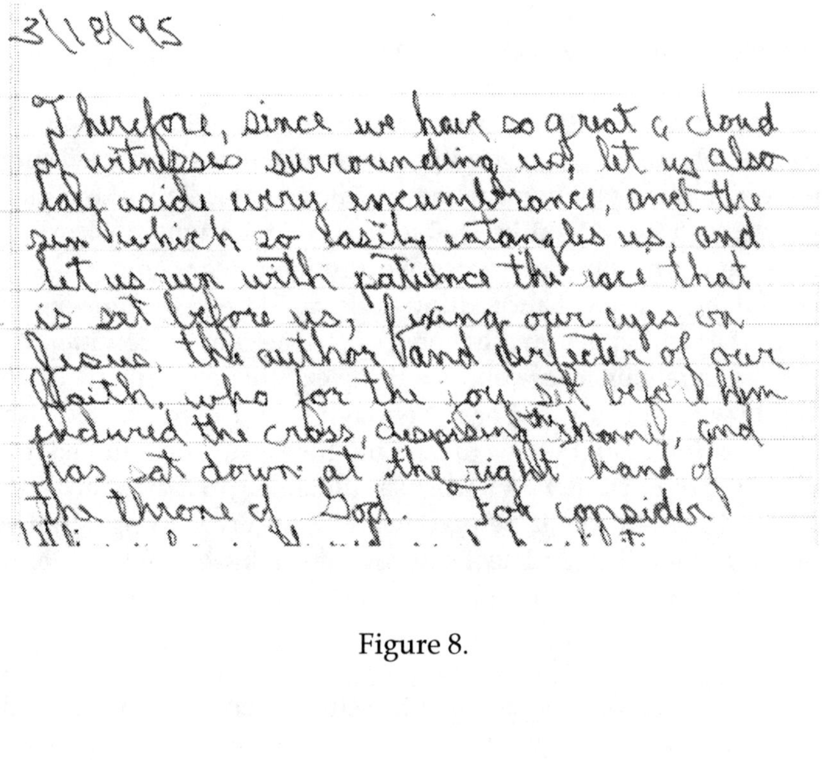

Figure 8.

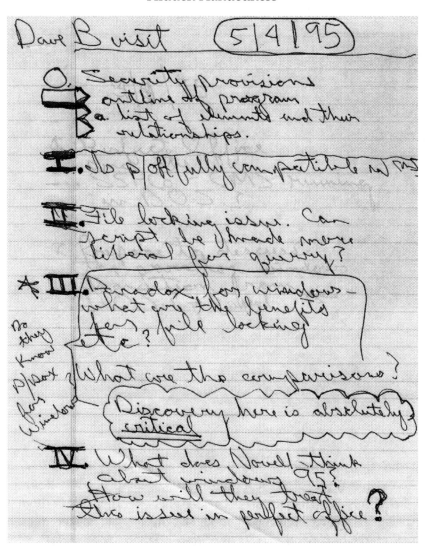

Figure 9.

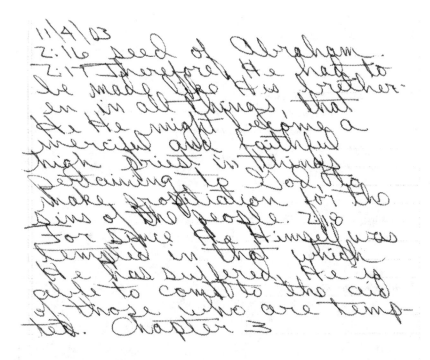

Figure 10.

I did find during my first year as an emergee that I would experience brief episodes of physical disorientation while writing. The momentary discomfort occurred whenever there was a mental struggle over a writing mistake. Examples of this confusion included what are referred to as *motorboat* letters. Motorboat letters are those in which reversals of looped letters, such as lower case cursive letters like *g*, *q* or *y* occur. Other letters that could trigger the same momentary sense of disorientation were the upper case letters *L*, *D* and *F*. Faulty letter slants, and mistakes made in the context of forming certain words, also triggered this kind of struggle.

I was inevitably challenged to write more quickly than I wanted to at work because of time pressures. After work, my practice sessions gave me the opportunity to write in a less frantic manner, enabling me to have a time of recovery during which I regained my sense of inner balance and satisfaction associated with writing. During work hours, if time pressures become too intense, I learned to deliberately slow down to the pace I used for my copying exercises. I would take a moment to write out a few carefully formed lines at exercise pace in order to get my writing back on track again. Using this deliberate centering process also helped me to remain aware of the many benefits of being an emergee while I was actively engaged in the work environment. My new perspectives and skills helped me to form new and more efficient work habits. This was an added bonus I hadn't expected.

I found that, in addition to mastering left-handed writing, a similar learning process was also at work in a host of other facets in my life where old assumptions and behaviors had formerly governed. For example, I had been swimming laps daily for more than ten years using a right-handed lead stroke to establish timing, breathing and stroke coordination. After emerging from my right-handed state, I substituted a left-handed lead stroke, which initiated changes that made swimming another venue for learning. The range of activities affected was surprising, including everything from simple movements like kicking, to more complex skills like handling a tennis racquet and the use of tools.

THE SOCIAL SETTING OF AN EMERGEE

None of the events I have been describing took place in a vacuum. Those I was are closest to were affected the most. The truth of that statement has been made clear by several close friends who have remarked that they are surprised our marriage could endure the many changes it went through at this time. Imagine a couple where one spouse goes through a non--stop mid--life crisis that endures for more than five years! Better still, imagine a situation in which one member turns into a strange mixture of an adult, a two-year-old child and an explorer all rolled into one. A few months of this kind of exposure would place significant strain on any relationship, but the process I have just described went on for years! Fortunately, I have a very understanding wife.

I was having the time of my life learning new skills, growing stronger and learning better ways of functioning, while exploring new perceptual horizons. With the enthusiasm of a child, I was re-discovering the world and learning about my self all at once. As these unexpected developments surfaced, not only did my wife *hang in there* with me through these years of intense transition, but she helped me develop an understanding of what had really taken place. It was as if she went *back to kindergarten* with me by being remarkably flexible, curious, open-minded, patient, and supportive.

Having recognized the important role my wife played, I also need to recognize the love and support I have been given as an emergee, both by my immediate family and by my wife's family. The value of this intimate and supportive circle of family became increasingly obvious to me as I grew and went through the inevitable process of ups and downs as I developed into my new identity.

The first need of an emergee will be for initial acceptance and personal support as they first begin to express their true identity. I was very fortunate to have the support of my family and those closest to me as I moved on as an emergee entering into the settings of society and business. A few words of affirmation spoken on my behalf in social settings proved to be terrifically important and encouraging. I learned something new about the value and the importance of having a positive social support system in place because, at times, I found that I truly needed the affirmation that came from my family and wife. Those who are near and dear to the one who decides to emerge, can play very important supporting roles.

I would like to take this opportunity to strongly suggest to anyone who is seriously considering taking the steps to become an emergee, that they enlist the help of their support system in advance. If the experience that I had is any indicator of what others might encounter in their own emergee experience, those who love and support them will have to deal with a significant and prolonged set of changes, many of which will be permanent as a part of the healing process. Those emergee candidates who are wise will hear my words of caution and include their loved ones in their decision-making process. I was very fortunate to have family members who accepted the new me and a wife who was willing to love both the old submergee, Sam, and the new emergee, Samuel.

I should add that some individuals who wish to become emergees may encounter resistance from their significant others. This is just one of many areas where psychologists and counselors will need to develop specialized expertise, because there will be a significant need for counselors and other specialized health-care professionals if large numbers of submergees decide to emerge. In addition to trained counselors, clinical services such as accurate and reasonably priced diagnostic testing will be needed. Health care professionals who are trained to interpret these tests and then discuss their implications with individual submergees will be needed to connect testing resources to end users.

LOOKING BACK

In order to make sense of my emergee journey and the events of submergee living that preceded it, I had to return "upstream" and analyze what had happened. Journaling, sharing with friends and family who were interested in my experiences, and even writing this book, have all been important parts of that process. Strangely enough, the passage of time has provided me with what I now see as the single most important learning tool I have had at my disposal in working to understand the essentials of the submergee and emergee issue. Years of development and growth had to be completed before the deeper perspectives I needed to work from had matured.

I realized within a few months of emerging that the ground I was covering in my *developmental spurt* **could only be crossed once**. Realizing that I had already started to forget what it was like to enjoy an unexpected emancipation from serious handicaps really bothered me. With that recognition, I felt, and still feel, a keen desire to retain the romantic and somewhat magical essence of what it was like to be an adult, who once again becomes a child passing through parts of the early developmental process. As the days of emergee living passed by, I found that my motivation to capture as much as possible of these very special days grew stronger.

MAPPING THE WORLD OF AN EMERGEE ~ CHAPTER 7

In this booming era of discovery, we have learned that the brain's neural networks respond in a pattern that is established by past experience; the more often a specific pattern is fired in response to a stimulus, the more firm the nerve assembly becomes. Hence the axiom: Neurons that fire together wire together. Input shapes the next input. It is not an exaggeration to state that after you have an experience, you are not the same person you were before the experience. Experience colors perception.[7]

John J. Ratey, M.D.

As right-handed *Sam* was transforming into left-handed *Samuel* I sensed that I was going home, and the picture of what the emergee experience consisted of gradually began to materialize. The terrain I was crossing became more familiar, and I realized that I was like an explorer who needed to develop a map of the virgin terrain through which I was traveling. On a personal level, this was a matter of survival. I also knew that if I could successfully record even some of the details of my travels, that other travelers like me might benefit from that record. My hope was that future travelers would be able to journey with far more comfort than I did, knowing that someone else had already passed that way. Landmarks are a wonderful solution when detailed maps can't be drawn. Landmarks must be large enough to be seen at a distance, and they must be carefully chosen, so they can be recognized and used at a later date by travelers who choose to follow the same route.

Landmark #1 -- The Physiological Foundation of Laterality

In searching for a reference system or "compass" that would provide a meaningful framework for my experiences, I looked to the field of neurophysiology and found a critical landmark: the

71

foundation of laterality, or what might be thought of as the "sidedness" of humans. I studied the two-sided physiology of the human nervous system. This structure or foundation, of the body determines the character of our handedness as well as the sidedness of many other parts of our being including the determination of which eye, ear, foot and function is preferred or dominant. Laterality, which forms the framework within which the functions of the left and right sides of the body operate, became a primary reference point, or pole star, which I could use with confidence to draw in the first outlines of a meaningful map.

Fixed reference points such as the pole star and related celestial points can serve us well when we are searching for simple yet reliable means of navigating with confidence in unfamiliar settings. A famous example of this process comes from the adventures of the Vikings who discovered the new world well before Christopher Columbus. In a variation on this theme, early Yankee sailors adopted an easy-to-use form of navigation that was based on celestial observations in lieu of the more complex chronometer-based method developed in England.

As I struggled to navigate successfully on the sea of emergee experience, I realized that because laterality was altered in the process of creating a submergee, and altered again in the return of an emergee, that gaining a clear understanding of the principles of this two-part system would be critical. As I started to draw my first maps of the submergee and emergee world, I realized the importance of the fact that the two-part neurophysiology that forms the foundations of handedness would serve as a concrete starting point. I had to keep in mind, however, the fact that laterality and the numerous systems of the human body and mind that operate within its context also represent one of the greatest puzzles in the universe.

The mystery of laterality is expressed in countless ways besides what can be seen in the neurology of humans. We see it at cosmic scales in categories such as the precise balance between matter and anti-matter. The principle of laterality applies to biological conundrums such as the twin strands of nucleotides that form the code for DNA. Some neuroscientists have argued that laterality is determined by molecular forces. At the smallest scales, subatomic particles are referred to by physicists in terms of their spin in one of two directions, a state which can be seen as a form of handedness. Laterality and the related principles of symmetry and asymmetry are at work throughout the created order. For a more detailed consideration of how laterality, symmetry, asymmetry and handedness are interwoven in humans and the world we live in, Professor Chris McMannus has produced an excellent overview of the topic in his encyclopedic book, *RIGHT HAND, LEFT HAND The Origins of Asymmetry In Brains, Bodies, Atoms and Cultures.*

The glorious fact that our nervous system is a two-sided structure that functions as if it were a unified entity sets the stage for questions and answers that speak to the design of that system. This physiological and functional framework governs neurological function in normal humans as well as in submergees and emergees, and as a single point of reference, it ties the experiences of all the handedness groups into a common setting.

The fact that we function within the physiological boundaries of a two-sided neurological system provides us with what is arguably our most important landmark of the body and mind. Starting with the two part structure which is the foundation of our handedness and laterality, we have a reliable starting point that provides a meaningful picture of the terrain in which submergees and emergees travel. By taking laterality as our starting point, we can begin to draw a meaningful and reliable map of what might actually be taking place in the body and mind of submergees and emergees.

Landmark # 2 –- The Point of Transformation and Departure

It is very difficult to adequately convey the sense of discomfort I felt when I first recognized how truly lost and alone I was as an emergee. Anyone who has ever had the experience of suddenly recognizing they are alone and have lost their bearings can understand the uneasy feelings that surface when this happens. I knew where I had come from (right-handedness) and where I wanted to go (left-handedness) but I was not prepared for what took place when I first stepped through the door of my left-handedness. I was like the person in the proverb who steps off a tall building and hears the warning on the way down *Watch out for that first step pal, it's a long one!*

I had passed through the emergee door and it felt like there was no bottom on the other side, no sense of why things should be the way they were. Dealing with rapid changes was something I knew how to handle, but the experience of being totally alone and without familiar reference points and reliable sources of information that I could rely upon was unnerving.

Consider what happened to me one morning, after two weeks of copying exercises and left-handed living. I woke up as usual and walked, half-asleep, into the bathroom. As I turned on the light and looked at the reflection in the mirror, I sensed that I was looking at a person I had never seen before. I wasn't frightened by what I saw, but there was enough of a difference that I was momentarily stunned. Looking closer, I could sense that something in my appearance had changed: then I noticed a light in my eyes that I had never seen before. It seemed as if there was a soft white glow within my eyes, almost as if they both had candles burning inside. I will never forget that moment: both scary and profound. I knew that *something important* had happened to me, but what was it?

Developmental discoveries like my strange experience with the mirror became commonplace. For example, I found the essential weirdness of the emergee experience itself was unsettling. The sense of *otherness* I lived with at this time is difficult to convey because as adults we exist quite comfortably within our familiar boundaries of self. At forty-one years of age, I was used to my submergee self and thus I found some aspects of the new emergee setting unfamiliar and uncomfortable. While a familiar setting is easy to live in, living in a novel one requires adaptation and the expenditure of considerable energy and effort. If, in the process of emerging, one's familiar surroundings are remodeled--or perhaps I should say, demolished and rebuilt it--stands to reason that the foundations of one's stability will most certainly be shaken. As I discovered, there are many real, intense, expensive--even exotic--experiences that are wrapped up in an emergee transformation.

As the pace of the initial emergee changes grew more intense, I found myself grasping for some sense of meaning, a vantage point that I could use in interpreting my experiences. Instead, I found that there was little to grab onto other than the newly revised facts of my history, plus prayer, faith, and my daily left-handed writing exercises. I was like a person adrift at sea in a life raft with no way of knowing his position. I needed something to help me place my experiences into perspective. I had to have maps and models of *what had happened and what might happen next* in order to navigate. I had no way to understand the meaning of the new world I was exploring, nor any means to predict what lay ahead.

Sometimes, the emergee growth spurts left me exclaiming *Oh my gosh!* My feelings were like the panic felt by someone riding on a roller coaster when the first really big drop looms into view. In these moments, I found myself far outside my comfort zone (the morning I encountered another person in my bathroom mirror is one example). Thankfully, I had an inner sense that all would be fine and, fortunately, the really intense changes came in a series of somewhat orderly and relatively comfortable progressions, one after another.

Because of the fast pace of the developmental process I experienced as an emergee, I now find the subject of transformations absolutely fascinating. I learned first hand that a series of seemingly trivial consecutive changes can in fact result in major transformation. As adults, we lose sight of almost all of the developmental experiences that we once lived through in childhood. We forget what it was like to be very small, because our transformative experiences took place so long ago. The millions of incremental changes, the series of wondrous steps that took us all the way from tiny babies to fully-formed adults are lost to us, but this portal remains ajar to emergees. The second landmark is one of departure and metamorphosis. The submergee who chooses to emerge must be willing to be transformed, to leave the familiar world behind.

Samuel M. Randolph

Landmark #3 -- Submergees and Alienation From Self

When a child is trained to become a submergee, they must undergo what amounts to an alienation from the form of self that their innate laterality determines. For numerous reasons, including the forces of culture, religion, ignorance and a wish to fit in on the part of the child or because of the personal preferences of adult guardians, the submergee child must accept the fact that their handedness, which is an essential part of who they are and how their brains are wired, is unacceptable. Restructuring and converting handedness alters essential components of the body and mind which is another way of saying that the child becomes someone they were not programmed to be.

In the process of accommodating the submergee state, the child's nervous system must preserve its pre-existing neural patterns and skills such as coordination of the muscles that govern eye movements and a host of other essential functions in spite of the fact that a transfer of dominance in the motor centers of the brain has taken place to support the challenge of writing with the non-dominant hand. The mind of the submergee child must accommodate the more complicated revised demands that are placed on the system by functioning in a less unified fashion, working in more of a split than unified fashion. Put in other terms, two "selves" are in some sense created by the unnatural functional demands which are placed on submergees. The dominant hemisphere which was once active is essentially denied volition as the weight of use of the dominant hand moves to the newly favored side. The submergee child becomes a different person, a unique and ghostly double is created within.

The submergee must learn to function in spite of the wholesale trauma that a shift in laterality represents to the nervous system. As submergee children adapt to the reality of their altered bodies and minds, they lose the efficiency of untrammeled nervous systems. They learn instead to use their bodies and minds in an extraordinary and altered manner and, in fact, they are themselves alienated and exiled to one degree or another in a different state than the one they would have lived in had they been allowed to be the people they were originally intended to become.

For a working analogy to the situation just described, consider the design of a typical ship, with its command center located on the bridge. The controls of a ship are placed in the optimal location for their intended use, situated exactly where the crew has the best possible access to sensory input and the systems that control the vessel. In like manner, the brain is *pre-wired* to express itself in its optimal state, one which is tailor-made to manifest the unique features of the individual's body and mind. If one day the doors to a ship's bridge were barred so that the captain and crew were denied access, they would be forced to operate the ship from an auxiliary control room located in a less than ideal position. The crew could still govern the ship's course from this alternate location in order to keep the vessel functioning, but there would be a significant loss in the precision, speed, and ease with which the ship could be operated.

Working from the auxiliary control room of the ship, the captain and crew must operate in an unnatural, cramped, and primitive space in contrast to the facilities that exist on the abandoned bridge. In the case of a submergee, he must transfer motor control over to his auxiliary hemisphere--an operational state which compromises the higher efficiency of his innate preferences, brain-wiring patterns, and previously learned skills.

For me, emerging was like reentering the bridge of my ship after years of being forced to operate from the auxiliary control room. Regaining access to my ship's bridge, working in comfort, with a splendid view and accurate controls at hand versus operating in a small, hot, dark and stuffy auxiliary control room was like being set free from prison and, at the same moment, learning that I was a wealthy man.

The process of alienation that I have been describing is captured nicely by a common piece of playground equipment, the teeter-totter. In this example, assume that each child sitting on opposite sides of the unit represents one of the brain's two hemispheres. If we wish to represent the hemispheric role for dominant handedness, it can be modeled by the heavier child, whose feet remain on the ground. In this context, the opposite hemisphere could be viewed in the role of the lighter child on the opposite side of the teeter-tooter, whose feet remain suspended in the air. The two children operate as one because they are joined together by the teeter-totter. Using this illustration to model what takes place when submergees are created, assume that enough weight is added to the side of the lighter child to reverse the balance. Now, the child whose feet were once touching the ground is lifted into the air. His feet are left dangling, and he is no longer the one whose feet are connected to the earth, no longer in charge of moving the teeter-totter.

In the analogy of the teeter-totter, the nature of the original pre-submergee self is altered by the submergee training process. The formerly dominant hemisphere (the heavier child) is moved into the subdominant role as the newly dominant hemisphere (the lighter child) gains weight and dominance because of greater use. When the submergee training is complete, the formerly dominant hemisphere of the submergee is still active, but left in an alienated state, like the child who suddenly finds his feet dangling in the air. Because primary motor control is now routed through the newly dominant hemisphere, volition and motor control are taken over by the formerly non-dominant hemisphere. Practicing submergee behaviors eventually creates habits that alter and re-configure the pre-existing balance between the left and right hemispheres. This alteration or re-setting of the teeter-totter of laterality creates a fundamental alienation in which the child is no longer fully himself or herself. The child becomes a submergee.

Landmark #4 -- Research Findings

Models of the mind that are based upon two distinct and yet complete hemispheres are now accepted as an accurate representation of the operating principles that shape the body and mind. Although the meaning of the phrase *hemispheric dominance* which we use in discussing the function of these hemispheres has different meanings depending on context, for the purposes of this discussion I am thinking in terms of laterality or weight-of-use for a given function such as handwriting and primary motor control of the body. The fact that the brain is organized within what are essentially two complete, collaborating operating systems makes any use of the term tricky, but necessary, since for operational purposes the body and mind choose to let one hemisphere lead, supported by the other, which follows.

A large body of evidence supports the fact that shifts in hemispheric dominance such as those that are experienced by submergees can and do occur. The thought that, in some sense, two minds exist in every human was viewed with wonder in the 1970's, when the work of Roger Sperry first became popular. Sperry's insights opened doors of interest and understanding and stimulated funding, research and thought on topics relating to laterality. Researchers addressing issues such as the *dual brain, interhemispheric transference of dominance*, the *bicameral mind* and a host of related subjects continue to expand the frontiers of what we know about the two-part body and mind.

Examples of research completed in the years following Sperry's pioneering work include a clinical investigation completed at the USC School of Medicine. Researchers at USC evaluated a subject who could voluntarily shift her cerebral dominance[8]. More recent studies completed in Germany have added important details to our understanding of the mechanisms that shape and enable the collaborative process of interhemispheric transfers.[9] Studies of patients suffering from Dissociative Identity Disorders (DID) have shown that alterations in identity or sense of self commonly include a concurrent shift in handedness and hemispheric dominance.[10]

Animal studies have shown that certain mammals can utilize a selective form of sleeping, in which one hemisphere rests, while the opposite hemisphere maintains consciousness. Using this unique strategy, certain birds, such as ducks are able to retain critical functionality; a state of vigilance against predators. Dolphins can continue to swim and breathe using this mechanism. A rich body of completed and ongoing research clearly illustrates the fact that transfers of hemispheric dominance and other equally complex behaviors linked to interhemispheric function take place in both animal and human brains.

Landmark #5 --Maps of Submergee and Normal Brains

The unique patterns of brain activation associated with submergee shifts in hemispheric roles have only recently been recognized by researchers utilizing Positron Emission Topography (PET) scanning equipment.[11] With recent developments in scanning technologies, a fresh landmark based on direct observation has come into view, one that enables us to compare the functional maps of normal brains and submergee brains.

In the research cited above a group of volunteers representing typical right and left-handers in addition to a group of submergees were evaluated. While the patterns of brain activation observed during handwriting were typical for the left and right-handed participants, the submergee group (defined in this case as left-handers who had converted to right-handed handwriting) demonstrated abnormal patterns of activation. Although the study did not look at right-handed submergees who were converted over to left-handed writing, it is likely that a similar abnormal pattern of use would also be observed in these submergees.

The key insight gained from this research is the fact that a persistent and abnormal activation of the right hemisphere remains in effect in submergee adults, in spite of the fact that the conversion took place many years ago. In the case of the submergees writing with their right hands, while the left hemisphere was actively processing the writing task as expected, the opposite right hemisphere also showed abnormally high activation levels. This pattern of brain use was not observed in the right-handed volunteers who were performing the same writing exercise with their right hands.

Comparing the three groups, right-handers and left-handers demonstrated the expected asymmetries of brain activation. In the case of right-handers, the left hemisphere was dominant, showing primary activity in the motor and related processing centers. The same patterns were observed in mirror fashion in the group of left-handers, in whom primary brain activity was observed in the right hemisphere. In using this study to draw a map of submergee brains, one would highlight the unusual activation patterns of submergees as a key landmark. In contrast to the normal brains of left and right-handed individuals, submergees operate in a unique fashion, maintaining a second operating system in addition to the primary operating system that governs movements of the writing hand.

Landmark #6--Conservation of Mind

The notion that a submergee mind functions by maintaining two active maps of reality, or what might be thought of in some sense as two working selves, flies in the face of commonly accepted wisdom about normal brain development and function. The use it or lose it axiom that applies to muscles also applies to neurons. Why pay the expense of maintaining redundant brain function? In the normal developmental progression, pruning of excess neurons takes place in two phases, first in early adolescence and again in the late teen years. For some reason, the submergee brain preserves neurons in the right hemisphere that should not be conserved.

Although the PET scan findings cited above need to be reproduced in additional studies for both handwriting and for other activity categories, the study's observations of abnormal dual hemisphere brain activity fit nicely in a model of the submergee mind that assumes conservation of the hard-wired skills that were learned prior to submergee conversion. PET scans show that an extensive array of neural networks located in the right hemisphere of submergee subjects continue to be accessed, ostensibly to provide guidance to the opposite hemisphere which is engaged in controlling the submergee's right-handed writing process.

In accord with the use it or lose it scenario for neurons, after a left-handed child has adapted to submergee function, the unused neurons in the right hemisphere should be converted to other purposes, not kept on line and actively engaged in an ongoing collaboration of hemispheres for tasks such as writing. However, based on the aforementioned PET scans, this very scheme of operation appears to provide the mechanism that makes handedness reversals possible. In order for submergees to function successfully, the redundant neural networks that would normally be pruned away must instead remain intact.

The PET scans of right-handed submergees engaged in a handwriting exercise showed unexpected activity taking place in the neurons of their right hemispheres. What purpose could be served by these extra neurons? Why weren't they identified as non-functional neurons by the developing brain and pruned away as one would expect? The sixth landmark in the landscape of laterality appears to have been sighted by a PET scanning device. This landmark points to the special operating systems at work in submergees, who maintain not one, but two functional operating centers in contrast to the more *asymmetrical* (dominant on one side and not both) single-sided style that is at work in normal brains.

If "input shapes the next input" as John Ratey asserts, then the unused neurons in the formerly dominant right hemispheres of submergee subjects must be serving some ongoing purpose. The inexplicable activity observed in the right hemisphere of submergees undergoing PET scans gives us the first pictures of a unique adaptation that apparently takes place in the submergee brain. The submergee's right hemispheres are actively doing something extraordinary in concert with the dominant left hemisphere that controlled writing in the right hand. If this observation is verified by further research, then submergee function breaks the use it or lose it rule at a very large scale. By the same logic, the emergee process must also break the rule when normal left-handed function is restored. The networks of neurons, or the resources that will be needed to support the development of enhanced motor skills in the body and mind of the emergee should not exist after years of disuse.

A principle I have referred to as *conservation of body and mind* appears to have been at work in me, guiding and governing the events of my submergee and emergee journeys. Somehow, the neural networks, my foundations of self, were conserved. Functioning as an emergee, my neural patterns shifted to approximate those of a left-hander, and through a combination of available neural resources and plasticity, a far more efficient and capable person emerged. Since neither hemisphere had to operate within the constraints of the inefficient submergee state, a rebound effect was evident. Once this emergee remodeling project was completed, I felt as if I was living in a new body and mind. So, is the principle of conservation of body and mind really at work in submergees? The answer appears to be *Yes*!

Landmark #7 --Rebound Effects

In my case, the emergee process resulted in enhanced function, not just a shift of handedness, which was all that I had expected to occur. The rebound effects I observed would require global plasticity of brain function that should not be possible at a late age. In my case these events took place at forty-one years of age, a time frame that was several decades removed from the period when myelination, or insulation of mature neurons has been completed. The rebound effects I experienced as an emergee point to an unforeseen process, one that researchers may wish to study. It would seem as if conservation of the body and mind is the governing principle, yet other mechanisms, including genetics, molecular influences on laterality, or forces that lie deeper still may be acting to guide the submergee and emergee process.

John Ratey comments parenthetically on the abnormality of enhanced emergee rebound in adults by speaking from the traditional neurological perspective.

Plasticity at multiple levels is more active in early life, so that damage at one site produces changes at many other sites, thus changing the brain and its functioning in a more widespread manner. In later life, with less capacity for remodeling at multiple levels, effects at a distance from the site of damage are less likely and specific deficits are more common. From mid-adolescence on, there is less rapid growth of new synapses that allow for flexibility and by then neurons are completely myelinated, or sheathed. Damage will cause deficits in specific skills with varying degrees of recovery.[12]

It appears as if the mind's ability to conserve neurons as required enables the submergee to preserve them in a functional state in spite of the cost of reduced operating efficiency that must be paid. This form of preservation seems to overcome the process of neuron pruning and limits on plasticity even after myelination is completed at a late age, by preserving an intact second operating system. If my map is correct, then this second operating system exists in mirrored form in the formerly dominant hemisphere of the submergee. If this mirrored cortex serves as a critical connection to hard-wired skills that must be maintained at all costs, then the submergee operating mode represents an operational compromise that makes the best of a difficult situation. In the case of submergees, two minds may well be better than one.

Landmark #8 -- Emerging = Going Home

The second operating system seen in the right hemispheres of the submergees in the German PET scans appears to serve the critical purpose of conserving the systems that also make the return journey of an emergee possible. The redundant system in the non-dominant hemisphere remains a functional part of the submergee's body and mind system. If the neurons of the redundant system were pruned, the event would be the equivalent of a tragic lateral lobotomy, a state of affairs that would preclude the potential for an emergee return. Fortunately, because the principle of neural conservation appears to be at work in submergees, the original wiring patterns of the brain are preserved intact instead of destroyed. Assuming that this outline is correct, the emergee process takes advantage of the marvelous plasticity of the body and mind, since a submergee's nervous system is in a sense *pre-wired* for this event. The operating axiom "Input shapes the next input," which governs the process that creates submergees, also seems to work in reverse in an even more powerful way, when an emergee homecoming takes place.

84

Thankfully for me, the neural pathways I had to travel on in order to emerge had been preserved. The original outlines of my left-handed self were clearly marked and available to guide me home on my journey. Thanks to the fact that the patterns formed in my earliest days were preserved in good standing for forty-one years, those guiding forces and talents remained intact. Early skills, from sucking the thumb to eye movement and a host of other learned behaviors of my body and mind, formed the foundations upon which I was built. It followed that the submergee operating systems, which had to be established in the opposite hemisphere, would have to function in an auxiliary fashion. The submergee system had to draw upon pre-existing core skills and patterns in my right hemisphere that could not be replaced or discarded

I felt that a greater hand than mine was at work in my life as I traveled down-river on my emergee exodus. The trip reminded me of migratory animals that are guided by mysterious yet precise instinctual mechanisms. Animals of all kinds have migrated successfully for millennia, exhibiting fascinating behaviors and traveling tremendous distances as a matter of routine. Somehow, I too was able to migrate safely within the confines of my body and mind. I exchanged a life where I functioned as a submergee, to the far healthier life of an emergee. I now view the navigational feats of migratory animals that are directed by what we glibly refer to as an instinctual guiding force, in much the same way as I see the process that guided me. My emergee journey home was instinctual and automatic to a degree that both fascinates and humbles me.

THE END OF THE RIVER ~ CHAPTER 8

This was the first use of her hands, her first manual act in sixty years, and it marked her birth as a "motor individual" (Sherrington's term for the person who emerges through acts). It also marked her first manual perception, and thus her birth as a complete "perceptual individual." Her first perception, her first recognition, was of a bagel, or "bagelhood" - as Helen Keller's first recognition, first utterance, was of water ("waterhood").[13]

Oliver Sacks, M.D.

As my first months of exploration turned into years of travel, I realized that the terrain I was now passing through had changed a great deal. Thinking in terms of a river journey taken by a kayaker, I had found my way far downstream. The banks were much further apart now, and the pace of the water's flow had abated. I was paddling smoothly, progressing along a broad channel as the many tributaries of my body and mind joined together to flow downstream in unison. I had gained a seemingly limitless supply of energy and new skills that encouraged me and added a little extra brightness to each day. In this stage of development, higher order skills such as emotional awareness and the improved social skills that should have appeared many years before started to mature.

From my perspective, the more complex skills that had taken months to develop arrived *out of the blue* as it were, in flashes of fresh insight and ability. Multi-sensory talents such as enhanced tactile, musical, and aesthetic awareness, along with a deeper sense of humor and a more mature emotional intelligence, flowed into my life, filling in the empty areas. To me, each new discovery was like a precious gift that I unwrapped with a sense of growing wonder. Each surprise was genuine, because I had no way of knowing that I had been living without the benefit of the abilities and sensory enhancements that became evident. With the gifts came a new awareness. I could now see that my submergee environment had been somewhat flat, lacking in the dimensions and colors I was now privy to as a matter of everyday experience. I could honestly say that the new awareness and sensory environment of *Sam the submergee* was sparse, limited and gray compared to that of *Samuel the emergee*.

Four months after beginning my emergee journey, an epiphany of sorts struck me while I was ensnared in heavy traffic in downtown San Francisco. As a submergee driver, these driving environments were nerve-wracking and frightening challenges that I secretly dreaded. I was headed north in daytime traffic in the outside lane on Van Ness Avenue and in the process of turning right toward the downtown, when the memorable *Ah ha!* Moment happened. The realization hit, *Hey, I don't need to be stressed out about getting into an accident!* From that moment on, my inner state changed in accord with the fact that I had become a far more relaxed and capable driver. The nervous and jerky style of driving that once made my passengers nervous and me afraid of getting into an accident was gone. Without realizing it, I had become a much better driver and this meant that I could relax and stop worrying about fears related to perceptual limits and awkward coordination. My secret dread of driving in the city had evaporated!

Five months after I emerged, I noticed that my visual system had begun to process information in a new way, incorporating a heightened awareness of information contained in the facial cues and expressions of others. In the course of a jobsite visit, I approached a group of construction workers who were sitting in a loose circle taking a break. As I approached the group, I was struck by the knowledge that I was able to read their faces and obtain information in a new way. I found this experience empowering and comforting, because now I didn't need to access information as I had in the past, by watching carefully for less accurate clues such as body posture. This newfound ability to instantly relate in a smooth and comfortable manner with complete strangers was exhilarating. During the long drive to and from the site, I realized that my driving posture had improved, requiring less energy. Searching for an explanation, I noticed that I had changed my posture as a consequence of switching from my former habit of driving with my left hand to driving with my right hand. That day, I returned home far less fatigued than normal after driving for ten hours.

Nine months after emerging, I abruptly became aware of the subtle information I was able to discern in the faces of female shoppers as I passed them in the aisles of a large crafts store. This second visual revelation, which came as a more detailed and powerful version of the earlier experience at the construction site, created a mild panic in me, as I realized that I now had access to far more information than I would have thought possible in this kind of exchange. I felt uncomfortable because I could again sense that something powerful had taken place, but this time I felt exposed. The insulated sense of existing in a more isolated and less accessible social space vanished. Not only was I able to access this new information, I also realized that I would henceforth be able to *speak* this new dialect. In spite of the fact that I knew this form of language had existed for others such as skilled poker players or those with finely tuned social skills, I had never understood it. I was now *reading* the facial expressions of each woman I passed at a level of detail that made that form of flirting both natural and possible for the first time.

A key insight that helped me to understand that I still had a long way to go in my emergee growth process came after more than four years of development. A significant Aha instant hit me while I was waiting for my wife, alone in our car, with time on my hands. As I was musing absentmindedly, the recognition that I was poorly equipped to connect emotionally with others struck me. In that moment, I could clearly see that in terms of social and empathetic development, I was, as I put it to my wife when she returned to the car, *emotionally retarded*. This awareness of my impoverished inner state flooded my mind as I replayed past experiences with this new understanding and recognized a number of my emotional deficits.

This process of recognition marked the beginning of a new phase in the emergee experience, as the kind of higher-order deficits I am describing became an issue that I recognized and worked to overcome. The events that followed were truly rewarding, because with awareness came development, sensitivity to my inner emotional world and to the emotional worlds within others.

The series of insights regarding further areas that needed growth continued to accumulate, resulting in fresh terrain to cross. Providing a detailed account of that process would easily fill a book, so please understand that the milestones I am sharing in this short chapter are limited in the interest of saving time and space. I would encourage anyone going through an emergee journey to journal the changes they observe for later review. Looking back from the perspective of four plus years, I came to understand that many of the advances which had been part of my earlier emergee development served to introduce me to higher-order pathways for growth. Following these newly discovered pathways by developing skills like improved emotional awareness would enable me to continue on my way, connecting my inner and external worlds in a more fine-grained and complete manner. This more mature set of skills also enabled integration of my newly enhanced senses and skills in a cumulative process. In this later growth phase where higher order skills were mastered and then integrated, it was as if I was finally learning to take a series of sequenced steps that enabled me to dance graciously, moving in harmony to a tune that I already knew.

The late developmental growth process I have just described in very limited detail unfolded over an extended period of time, and it still continues to this day, but at a much slower pace. I keep returning to the metaphor of a river journey because of its similarity to the ongoing and progressive nature of the emergee process. In that context, the initial rapid changes of emergee growth took place in a flood surge, one that rushed along between narrow riverbanks. With the passage of time, I found the emergee process opening up into a much more comprehensive experience, one in which the abilities mastered in the past were combined synergistically, integrated and growing in power and scope, in the same way that rivers grow in size and depth as they run into the ocean.

It is tempting to report on my journey as if it were one continuously unfolding event that flowed along without interruption; in reality, the most memorable parts seemed to happen suddenly, with bursts of insight, moments when significant changes became apparent or new avenues of growth opened up. As these memorable mileposts passed, each one helped me to understand the fact that far more was taking place than I could be aware of. Important changes and transformations had already taken place, needed to take place and were continuing to take place in connection with the process I was engaged in. Lots of little and seemingly insignificant alterations were assembled together to become a series of big changes. I was growing up fast.

I believe that the more complex skills I have described began to function much more fully after several years of emergee growth, because the systems that were needed to support their function finally matured and integrated. A metaphor for what had happened at this stage might be the completion of an important network of freeway bridges in a densely populated area that suffers from gridlock. Once those key bridges are opened up, traffic that needed access to the more efficient connections will be able to flow in a far more rapid and efficient manner. To the uninformed observer, the process of constructing such a system might seem to be a meaningless endeavor, because so many small and seemingly unimportant sequenced phases of work are required to complete complex and large-scale projects. But to those who ultimately get to experience the difference between gridlocked traffic and the routine of efficient travel, the years of effort are well worthwhile. The changes that our metaphorical traveler experiences once the bridges are opened up are no less profound than the altered environment I entered into as I moved from submergee to emergee status.

Recent findings in neuroscience support the understanding that plasticity and the capacity to accommodate neurological change exists in humans from birth to death. This life-long ability will be illustrated rather dramatically if we discover that the emergee experience is yet another, albeit much delayed and accelerated, developmental processes that exists within the repertoire of the changes that humans can accommodate. We now know, for example, that the neurological wiring process that takes place as the prefrontal cortex of the brain matures can continue to occur as late as thirty years of age. In my case, rewiring of the systems that would support higher-order function and integration had to be completed even later, beginning at age forty-one.

To provide an overview of the developmental transitions I have reported on, I would say that the most radical changes I experienced took some two years to unfold. Many of the early changes were physiological in nature, such as the massive improvements in visual and auditory efficiency I experienced. What I refer to as the higher-order skills required three additional years to develop and one of these late developing skills was in fact an improved sense, which was a much greater tactile awareness. As I write, I am looking back from an eleven year perspective, one which gives me a fairly good grasp of the events I am reporting on. With the advantage of hindsight, it is clear that there is no way I could have written about emerging in any complete sense at the two, three or even four year mileposts subsequent to emerging. A four year window was needed before enough pieces in the emergee puzzle had fallen into place. It was at that point that I began to write in hopes of sharing my story with others with a growing sense of understanding and confidence. As I look ahead, there are many new territories that I have yet to explore, but these are primarily connected to the larger concerns of submergees and emergees, the social and scientific issues that need to be addressed.

Once my emergee journey down-river was essentially completed at about five years, I found that I was living my life far more completely. I was Samuel, a different person who operated in a new world. Like a bird free to fly the open skies for the first time, the prison cage that had confined me was gone. The process of gaining my new bearings and finding my way in the wide world required patience, understanding and integration, a linking of the world of my submergee past with the growth, opportunity and changes of daily life. I was equipped to enter into life in a new and richer way. The tools that were now mine to use because of the emergee growth process had made my new version of adulthood a much more multi-faceted and complete one.

In the stories of an adult emergee that follow, I will share some of my experiences with you. These stories took place as I began to develop revised understandings of myself, and the new world that I had discovered.

STORIES OF AN EMERGEE ~ CHAPTER 9

I am Bob Randolph, Samuel's brother, senior in age by two years. In addition to growing up together, we have also worked together for much of our lives. For the past fifteen years we have worked in adjacent offices while involved in the business of introducing and selling new technologies for environmental and construction-related applications. This is a fairly technical undertaking that involves a considerable amount of written communication. My responsibilities include reviewing and editing the more important written communications that are sent out by our company, so I have spent considerable time reviewing Samuel's correspondence.

I am particularly sensitive regarding the quality of written communication produced by our business, hence I admit to being a rigorous editor. It is in the area of Samuel's written communications that I most clearly recognized a significant change occurring during the immediate period of his switching from being a right-hander to left-hand operations. His written output improved noticeably. While he was never what I would describe as a poor writer, the formation of his sentences and the logical flow of his presentation often required considerable editing during the seven previous years. Following his transition, Samuel's writing almost immediately improved to a level where very little editing has been required.

While it was also my observation that Samuel became more effective in his overall work product and productivity following the switch of handedness, it was the concurrent improvement in the quality of his writing that made it apparent to me, without a doubt, that he was now thinking and processing more clearly and was able to articulate his written communications with noticeably improved logical flow.

Bob Randolph 8/15/03

One of my most enjoyable activities as a writer has been the process of revisiting my history of transition in stories. I knew that

I needed to capture the recent past in a narrative form that would convey something, some first-hand sense of the special experiences I had while moving from one world to another, from submergee to emergee status. In composing these stories of an adult emergee, I have had a special privilege, the chance to see a fascinating set of past experiences with fresh eyes.

Ground Zero

I am driving by myself, headed south on California's Highway 101 on a Friday evening in summer. I am traveling to meet my wife Tralee in Santa Cruz after a long week of work. I feel very pleased to have arranged this rendezvous with my wife at a destination a few hours away from our home.

I am driving a white SUV that gives me a good view of traffic ahead and to the side as I pass a line of slower moving traffic on my right. Up ahead in the right lane, I notice another white vehicle, a large commuter van carrying a full load of passengers.

Well, it's been four years since you found out the truth about yourself, I think. The difference in the mental space I exist in now as an emergee, compared to the one I experienced as a submergee, is hard to believe. At age 45, I feel as though I have lived a whole extra life in just three years. With an unexpected flash of insight, I see many of the positive consequences that the changes of the recent past have brought into my life. I feel incredibly rich, blessed beyond words.

Look at the way your mind is working right now, I say to myself. *Now you plan ahead, visualizing your world from a more global and powerful perspective. Your planning process is different, both in terms of space and time. The kind of a rendezvous you have arranged for today is totally new, something you never did before.* I am moved by this insight, realizing that most of the changes which have made this possible have taken place outside my awareness. It feels to me as if I have just awakened from a dream, one in which I was liberated without effort, automatically pulled up out of the pit I had been trapped in and sent joyfully on my way.

I am elated at the unexpected richness of this enhanced world. *What a gift of life! Why should I be so fortunate to have this strange but wonderful experience? Why me? I've done nothing to deserve this, what made me so special?* I know the reason this moment is mine to experience results from the simple fact that my desperate prayer was answered, *Why must I suffer from mental handicaps for the rest of my life?* It was exhilarating to realize that my request had been answered in a way that I would have never dreamed possible.

Like Narcissus gazing at his reflected image in the still water, I am nearly lost to the world for a few seconds as these thoughts play out in my mind. In the meantime, I have begun to slowly pass the white van. Our vehicles are side by side when I shift my gaze to the right. I can see the passengers' faces clearly, and I am caught off guard by what I see. The van is filled with young men who are sitting passively, slack jawed and staring straight ahead as if each one is in a trance. In this state of mind, I automatically visualize myself riding in the van. For a moment, I am one of the disabled passengers. I am dazed by the strong sense of empathy I feel, while at the same time I am struck by the dramatic difference between my new world and theirs. For a moment, the truth of what I have been set free from overwhelms me.

My years of living in a mentally disabled state automatically link me to the young men sitting in the van. I had lived with struggles that made me an outsider, and in my heart I still identify with each passenger. I had worked hard as a submergee to compensate for my deficits, driven by the sense that I must learn to pass as a normal person. Memories of the many times I was called *weird* or *out of sync* or even *spastic* crop up in this moment.

As the van falls away to the rear, I sense that I am leaving a part of my past behind with it. In truth, the encounter served as a personal touch point that I will never forget.

My encounter with the van was a "Ground Zero" moment for me because it did what words could not do. The shock of re-connecting gave me the incentive I needed to tell my emergee story in spite of my natural reluctance to share personal matters publicly. When I need motivation to continue the work of sharing my story, I can return to this scene to regain my sense of just how fortunate I am. They will never know it, but these young men gave me the gift of inspiration I needed to begin the work of reaching out to others like me.

THE PROSE OF A SUBMERGEE

On the evening of June 26, 1993 I had an experience that almost seemed like a vision. I was in that drowsy state between dreaming and being fully awake when this happened. At the time that my poem "The Prisoner" was written, I was still nineteen months away from the *Emergee Aha!* of March 5, 1995. I realized at the time that the visual scenes portrayed represented a special artistic window of opportunity, so I sat down and jotted the few lines that follow in an effort to capture what had happened and the words that captured the experience came pouring forth. The intense emotions that accompanied this encounter had a lasting impact.

The Prisoner

The dingy room is very quiet where he lays quietly, alone
His face is indistinct . . .
I can see the signs: several weeks of unshaven beard
rumpled tee shirt, eyes in dark circles
Now he senses my presence
I hear the rustle of bed sheets

The man is sitting up, getting closer because he wants to look at me
Without a word, curiosity is evident in his body language
He moves again to the table, across the floor
getting nearer, certain that he is not alone

I am afraid
What can I do?

I had a strong sense that this experience was important, because the poem was rooted in a type of visual impression that was new to me. I don't write prose regularly to this day, but this abnormal, almost supernatural confrontation made enough of an impact on me to elicit the response of writing about it. Now, as I read the verses years later and recognize the way the vision prefigured what was about to take place, I am struck by the manner in which it describes the behavior of the imprisoned left-handed character trapped within submergee Sam.

JS Finds A Support Group

JS's favorite toy is a wooden bee with yellow plastic wheels and wings that spin around as he pulls it across the polished wood floor. As JS plays on the floor, his Grandmother and parents are watching. Grandmother is frowning with her arms crossed as she sways back and forth in her rocking chair.

Grandmother says to Mother, *That poor child is going to grow up to be just like me; left-handed and wishing he could be right-handed like everyone else! You'll want to train him as soon as possible to be right-handed, like all of the other children with whom he will be growing up.*

You know, says Mother, *I heard that Dr. Spock, the famous pediatrician recommends that parents switch their left-handed children if possible to spare them the trauma of being different. I had no idea that it was so bad being left-handed and I can see how that could be a problem for our child too. It looks like he'll be left-handed to me too. If Dr. Spock says that switching a child to be right-handed is good for them, it sounds like it would be a good idea to do that for our JS.*

JS pulls his bee over to the side of Grandmother's rocker. As she leans over to pat her Grandson on the back, the relief is evident in her voice as she says, *Let me assure you, dear, you will be doing the very best thing for JS. No one should be forced to live as I have, doing everything backwards, simply because they have no choice. Believe me, being forced to use tools that make you look like a clumsy idiot, and then cramp your hand, is just horrible. The world just isn't made for left-handed people and I suffered every day in the salon because of it. I wish I could cut hair properly, but instead I have had to put up with this silly right hand that can't cut hair. After awhile he'll get used to being right-handed just like my son did and then he'll be fine when he grows up. I only wish I had been trained to be right-handed too, but I'm too old for that now.*

Forty-five years later, another conversation is about to take place. I have been invited to speak about my experiences to a group of eight elementary school counselors. The occasion is the groups meeting for the month of September. The year is 1999 and we are seated around a table in a small conference room. The counselors are an even mix of men and women, most of whom are seasoned professionals. I feel welcomed in this informal setting, and as the meeting opens I have everyone's undivided attention, because of the subject I am about to share.

I'll start at the beginning when I was switched or trained to become right-handed. It's important to understand that, until 1995, just four and a half years ago, I was convinced that I was right-handed. I brushed my teeth, wrote, threw, kicked, played tennis, golf and other sports as a right-hander. I was convinced at a young age that I was a bona fide right-hander and if it weren't for my strange 'awakening' experience, I would still be living as if that assumption were true. I am strongly left-handed, so I really was a fake right-hander.

I started to struggle academically as soon as school started. My problems became chronic in first grade, a period of time I have very few memories of. I was almost held back in first grade. As I grew older, I learned to 'pass' or fit in more successfully with my peers. Beneath the surface, I was struggling with chronic depression, a poor self image, and learning disabilities. Both my older and younger brothers had much different experiences.

In early January of 1995, almost five years ago, I was moved to pray earnestly and ask God 'why' I had to live in what I had learned to refer to as a mentally handicapped state I thought of as 'compensated dyslexia.' I knew that something serious was wrong with me, but I had no idea that there was a cure for my problems. As I prayed, I received a definite sense of comfort, a deep peace and knowledge that larger purposes were really being served because of my life experiences.

Hidden Handedness

Two months later, on a Sunday afternoon, March 5, 1995, my mind was inspired in a unique manner. The moment came for me as I was alone, practicing tennis against a backboard. Hearing a difference in the movement of my feet as I played right-and then left-handed, I suddenly just knew *that I was a lefty.*

At that time, I would have rejected any one else's suggestion that I was really left-handed. Fortunately, I was the one who stumbled upon the clue. My suspicions were immediately affirmed, first by my wife and then by both of my parents. Mom explained that they had started training me to become right-handed when I was about one year old. She told the story of Grandmother Randolph's early observations that I was left-handed and her recommendation to reverse my handedness.

I am amazed at how accepted and supported I feel as I share in this setting. Now one of the female counselors shares her thoughts.

As a counselor, I have to deal with situations where parents or teachers are forcing children to switch their handedness. If in our opinion, these reversals are creating a problem, how do we tell the child's parents to stop abusing their children? We have no effective way of communicating the problems the parents are creating for their children. You really need *to write your book for us and for the children that continue to be impacted. How soon can you get your story into print?*

I answered her question:

Only a few weeks ago I received a similar exhortation from Dr. Oliver Sacks when he responded to my letter asking for his help in telling this story. Dr. Sacks is a neurologist who specializes in the study of unique human experiences like mine. When I wrote him to ask for help in getting the story out, he admitted his interest, but said that he really had no time to spare for the project. Strangely, his words echoed yours. Dr Sacks wrote back and advised that I should *write a book length account of my experience. Apparently autobiographical accounts written about topics like mine are very rare. Now I am faced with a choice, to write that book or remain silent. In my heart I no longer have a choice.*

Once I knew that I really was left-handed, it seemed as if there was no option but to become the person I was been born to be. I had no idea of the huge changes I was about to unleash by making this simple choice. I thought, This change may take a few minor adjustments, but nothing major. *I learned subsequently, that I am in fact, strongly left-handed, so for me, the return trip from right-handedness to my native handedness was a significant one. Without realizing it, I had pulled the cork out of the bottle that had kept me trapped in my reversed handedness. The best explanation I can offer for the intense changes that followed is that by choosing to become left-handed, I reversed the assumptions and habits that had kept me bottled up, thinking of myself and functioning as a right-hander.*

From the day I learned that I was left-handed, I stopped using or preferring my right hand for writing and for other skilled tasks, <u>period</u>. This was sort of a cold turkey *change for the right hand, but I am convinced now that it was exactly what I needed to do.*

Just as important as making changes in my behavior, I began to see myself as a different person, a left-hander. I had a new vision of myself. As soon as I realized that I really was left-handed, the healing and integration process began.

I signed my checks, opened doors, threw balls, ate, drew, and even brushed my teeth and shaved using my left hand. You could truthfully say I was obsessed with being who I really was and discovering what I had lost. I had a sense of deep and abiding joy that was affirming and energizing. This was an obsession I could live with, but it is also an area for caution, because the number, strength and duration of the changes eventually became a problem for my wife. She had to deal with the new me. I had become a different person than the one she married.

I spent a minimum of an hour every day learning what it was like to write in cursive style with my left hand. The copying exercises gave me a sense of confidence and stability that served an important purpose at this time. My source was the Bible, which has inspiring verses, numbering and flawless grammar that makes it perfect for this purpose. As I worked, I sometimes noted a momentary sense of dizziness that became apparent to me whenever I slanted the letters too far back or forward. I realized that these momentary disorientations were simply a part of the process of gaining a fresh focal point or center from which to operate my mind and body and that the copying exercises were a critical part of the learning process.

At this point in our visit, one of the men interrupts me to offer his thoughts in the form of a question. *So, are you saying that what happened to you was something like an amputation of a limb, or in your case, a part of your mind?*

Exactly! I respond. *Only the experience took place <u>without</u> surgery, because for sake of conversation, I would say that a child whose handedness is reversed* moves out *of their dominant hemisphere in some manner when their laterality is re-set in this way. The end result is a human being who has in some sense suffered an amputation of mind or what one of my friends once referred to jokingly as a* lateral lobotomy. *I would say that in my case, the consequences of returning to left-handedness might be compared to the process of having this* lateral lobotomy *reversed.*

As time passed, I would say that a number of my developmental sequences started to operate again in spite of the fact that I was forty-one. I was surprised to note physical changes within the first two to six weeks, like a change in my wrist size and finger musculature. Soon, I <u>had</u> to start wearing my watch on my right arm, because it interfered with my writing and because the left wrist had grown large enough that the watch band was too tight.

Many of the changes I observed happened unconsciously. Most notable, my left eye became my dominant eye instead of my right eye. The most powerful physiological change followed that shift; I developed a much sharper and richer visual system. An example of this change was the discovery that I was able to write perfectly straight lines without using lined paper.

I recall at the time the sense of having gained back fifteen or twenty years of my life. The intense excitement of discovery made everything in my life seem new. It was as if the wattage of the lamp inside of me had been turned up, melting away all of the old disabilities.

Samuel M. Randolph

I would rank the loss of low-level chronic depression as one of the best changes of all. Being set free from depression was especially poignant, because I had struggled with a desire to commit suicide during my most serious episodes. The "minor" weight of chronic depression had been one of the handicaps that I struggled with without realizing it, never knowing where it had come from or why I should have to carry it.

Like anyone who makes a major personal change, I wanted to find others like me. The discovery that I was a solo act was an unpleasant surprise. I have yet to learn of anyone who has told the story of his or her emergee experiences. On a positive note, the painful situation I found myself in has made it clear that I need to share my story with others.

After I decided that I would tell my story, I realized that my hesitation had served a good purpose. The changes that began on March 5, 1995 hadn't stopped at two or three years, nor could I even begin to understand their meaning in a shorter time span. After three years, it became clear that a one or two year perspective would be insufficient. I learned to respect the need for patience and in fact this meeting with you today is the very first time I have shared my story formally.

To leave you with something special to remember, I would like to tell you a story about a young tree in a wild green forest. Many years ago, this healthy tree was transplanted after a forest fire. Unfortunately for the tree, the person who moved it was in a hurry and he relocated it from its original sunny spot to a shadowy and dry part of the forest. Because of the poor setting, most of the young tree's limbs died, and its roots were stunted by the lack of sunlight and parched soil. Many seasons of winter and summer pass, and what was once a healthy young tree growing up in the very best part of the forest, becomes a poor specimen, an unhealthy tree with a few scrawny green twigs.

One day in the fall, a naturalist is wandering about and studying the forest. She notices the poor stunted tree and decides to transplant it to see what happens. As fortune should have it, she wisely moves the tree back to its original sunny spot! By the following spring, the healing process is well underway. The unimpeded sunshine reaches the tree, warming and energizing its bark and leaves. The tree has ample access to water and the rich nutrients it was meant to have. The sun shines without any hindrance, supplying its power to the roots which reach down deep to draw up fresh water. The gentle breezes now blow on each branch, enabling the green needles to open wide and breathe in the invigorating air.

The tree knows exactly what to do, and it grows and grows, rising swiftly into the sky in a migratory process from stunted dwarf to healthy maturity. In spite of its horrible past, the tree now participates fully in the web of life at work in the healthy forest. For those with the senses to hear it, there is a joyous song of life in this forest that teaches the hearer how to respect and understand the beauty and patterns of life that are at work there. Every year the young tree's thankful song is heard with delight by the naturalist as she pauses to admire the song of one of her favorite trees in the forest.

The end.

Our time is up, so we end with a few quick questions before I exit the room. As I walk to my car, I return again in my mind to the scene of little JS. I am little JS (Junior Submergee). I can hear the conversation between my Parents and Grandmother once again, but this time, something has changed. Now I am in the company of an encouraging group of elementary school counselors who have taken the time to understand this story. I can sense the group's warm encouragement and support. I sense that I am no longer alone as I leave the school, and I know that I have a very special story that must be told.

AN EMERGEE DETECTIVE SETS OUT ~ CHAPTER 10

Being Samuel's brother, I always thought he was very creative. While growing up together I remember our shared bedroom. He had created a very involved experiment with a string tied to the door handle. When someone opened the door the string relaxed and was attached to every kind of thing you could imagine. The experiment created a cascade of things happening. Needless to say, our room looked like a spider web of strings and devices that all sprang to life when someone opened the door.

One day many years later while Samuel was practicing tennis on the backboard, he switched from right hand to left hand--something clicked inside him. All of a sudden he didn't feel so awkward in his stroking the ball and footwork. A little light had gone off, so he decided to call Mom and Dad and ask if he had been a switched left-hander at a young age. Confirming that he had been switched on-purpose by parents and teachers, a mystery of life began to emerge such as The Odyssey or the Iliad, or one of Marco Polo's journeys.

Just as the opening of the door caused the string to release the cascade of events, this change from forced right-handedness to natural left-handedness has been life changing for him and for many others around him.

Paul Binford Randolph - 7/9/03

When I was five years old, one of my very favorite games was Super Hero. Each of us would borrow an old terry cloth towel from our mom and then use it to make a cape formed with a diaper pin clasp at the neck. As soon as I was in costume, I could fly and had super powers. Our heroes were Batman, Superman, and the Green Lantern. I thought the Green Lantern was especially cool, because I could be dressed for action with my cape and one of Dad's paper cigar rings. Twenty or thirty minutes of super hero power was better than eating ice cream!

I Sam, grew up and learned to live as an adult who didn't have the time and freedom of expression that it takes to be magic and playful. Ironically, as I look back and read the earliest journal entries I wrote as a forty-one year old emergee, I am reading the words of a family man who has again entered into the stuff of super hero magic and play. My journal entries are filled with thoughts like this: *If I share the reality of my emergee experience, it will seem as if I was playing an adult version of Super Hero! Perhaps hyperactive imagination sparked an adult fantasy of a return to my past, or I was on drugs, or abducted by space aliens. People will think I'm crazy!*

One word that stands out in the journal is *shocked*. I write that I am *shocked* that the learning disabilities I had struggled with all my life are gone. I am *shocked* that the dandruff I had since fourth grade has gone away of its own accord. I am *shocked* that I can hear eight or more parts in complex music instead of just three, and *shocked* that I only need six hours of sleep instead of eight. As these changes-and a host of others--appear in my journal, I am unable to explain any of them without referring to my new left--handed identity. I am reminded of my childhood experience of putting on my super hero cape, only I am no longer five years old. My new powers are real this time and I am elated, to put it mildly. In looking back, I can tell that something phenomenal has happened.

THE SEARCH BEGINS

I was confident that there must be an expert or two out there who could tell me what had happened. I fully expected that these experts would be able to offer me the detailed guidance I needed. With their help, I would learn what I should do next. As I knocked on every door where an answer might be found, I began to get the uncomfortable feeling that nobody was home. My hope that I would find experts on handedness reversals wasn't going to be realized. Instead, I learned that I had stumbled into some kind of a phantom terrain, a place without maps that didn't exist in the real world.

Unless I wanted to resort to hyperbole or exaggeration, it seemed as if there was no way to explain what had happened without evoking disbelief or polite disinterest. I hadn't thought that it would be so difficult to convey to others the essence of the alien state I now found myself living in. A big part of the difficulty I faced in sharing my experience arose from the fact that the important changes I most wanted to share were taking place internally. Others could never truly see the tremendous difference between the internal *before* picture of me living as a submergee and the *after* picture that would portray the reality of my new life as an emergee.

Because I had no map to show me the many unexpected twists and turns that lay ahead, I couldn't *Just get used to it and get on with my life* as if nothing had happened. First, a *miracle* or *rebirth* of this magnitude was a really big deal if I was any judge of human experience. Second, without the reference system or map that connected my powerful and mysterious journey to the experiences of others, where could I go to relate the details of that journey to others? Where were all the people who must have gone through an emergee experience like mine? Who could I speak to besides family members and close friends without sounding like a bore or a madman?

Coming from a Scottish background, we were taught to respect the power of books, research and hard work. I was raised to believe in the power of resources like libraries and in looking to experts if there is an especially difficult problem to solve. I harbored an ingrained belief that answers were fairly easy to find for those who knew how to use the right tools and then applied themselves diligently in their search for understanding. In addition to the library, I had access to the Internet, which at the time was emerging as a form of a super intelligence that could be used to ferret out clues to unknown or arcane topics. Surely, the answers I sought would be found with a little effort? I wasn't prepared to discover that my hopes were misplaced.

With time, I began to realize that ready answers to my questions were not going to be found. I had to accept the limited information that was available, and have faith that eventually I would learn more. As I gathered a larger perspective by gradually putting together varied sources of information, I realized that I would have to adjust my views on what I should expect to accomplish. I needed to accommodate the unexpected lack of resources by recasting the world I was exploring as one where experts just did not exist. I would have to explore areas that others had avoided or overlooked.

In the first six months of my search, the person who came the closest to being an expert was Donald Joy PhD. Dr. Joy very kindly responded to my letter seeking insight into the subject of handedness reversals with a phone call in July of 1995. Although it was disappointing to learn that Dr. Joy didn't have research or experts to refer me to, his candor and encouragement were refreshing. He wisely advised that I should continue to *Go with my wiring* and become fully left-handed. In other words, this one who was the closest thing to an expert that I could find told me that he was *Happy for me* now that I had chosen to become left-handed again, and he advised that I would do well to continue with the process.

Six years passed before I read *The Left-Hander Syndrome: The Causes and Consequences Of Left-Handedness* written by Professor Stanley Coren, of the University of British Columbia. Coren reviewed the topic of handedness reversals in the larger context of left-handedness, summarizing available research, and performing surveys focused specifically on the question of handedness reversals. Coren writes on page 68 of *The Left-Hander Syndrome:*

Although many people offered opinions on this matter, we were surprised to find little work that looked at changing handedness. *This lack of information meant that we would have to collect the data ourselves.*[14] (emphasis mine) Others--including Harold N. Levinson, MD, psychiatrist, author, researcher and therapist specializing in the field of dyslexia and learning disabilities--confirmed the statements of Dr. Joy.

Oliver Sacks, MD wrote back and he too affirmed the feedback of Donald Joy and Dr. Levinson. Essentially, all the experts with whom I had direct contact said, *There are no experts in the area of handedness reversals.* I had the letter from Sacks framed, and keep it close enough to look at as I work because I still find his words encouraging and insightful. Writing back to me on August 20, 1999, Sacks says:

Many thanks for your intriguing letter. What you described, with recovery of your own "natural" left-handedness, is remarkable and I think you should tell the story. How much relevance, or "resonance" this would have for others (for there must be many, as you see, who have been "forced" into right-handedness, with some neurological problem in consequence) I cannot tell nor do I know whether such "transformations" have been experienced by others.

The letter from Sacks put an end to my doubts. Somehow, I had to find a way to tell the submergee story.

I Take The Case

With the words of the experts to spur me on, I borrowed a page from the cosmologists and began my hunt for the Big TOE--or *Big Theory Of Everything*--regarding the submergee and emergee story. I had already taken the first step in cracking the case by studying up on the topic of neurology and laterality. I was fortunate to find a good introductory text called *Left Brain, Right Brain* by Sally P. Springer and Georg Deutsch. Equally fortuitous was the fact that the resources of the Internet were available. Thankfully, the excitement I needed to spend long nights learning remained strong because my curiosity was insatiable, and the Internet rewards those seeking information. It also served as a valuable window into the diversity of research, opinion and controversy that surrounds the subject of handedness and laterality.

The first clue fell into place when I found that the subject I was studying was tremendously complex and poorly understood. John Horgan wrote rather tellingly about the limits of what neuroscientists really know in his book, *The Undiscovered Mind* (1999). Further, I learned that many competing theories regarding laterality and the related systems of the human body and mind abound in the absence of a single widely-accepted model. Complicating matters, the Internet-driven explosion of global knowledge has overwhelmed us, delivering massive quantities of new information regarding laterality and handedness.

In the short span of ten years, the difference between what was known then and now has proved to be critical. In addition to the general growth of knowledge in this category, several key insights on the mind were published within the years just prior to the completion of this book. The fortuitous timing of my search contributed greatly to its success. Had I attempted to form an understanding of submergees and emergees just ten to fifteen years earlier, before understandings of a plastic and dynamic body and mind were revealed by research, my story would have seemed very far-fetched, and equally important, unsupported by science. It was indeed a rewarding time to search for clues.

I needed to develop a reasonable understanding of our bilateral makeup before I could hope to work productively on deeper questions relating to submergee and emergee function. Questions like the nature and purpose of the two-part human brain provoked me. Why, for example is the mind biologically *bilateral* (or physiologically a two-sided organ) but functionally asymmetrical? The sub-dominant hemisphere is often portrayed as something of an abyss, a part of our minds we fear, much as we fear death. This same sense of mixed wonder and fear applied to many of the questions I was asking about handedness and laterality. My question seemed as if it should be simple to answer: *What physiological changes take place when a human's preferred handedness is reversed and later restored?*

In 1976, Julian Jaynes of Princeton University presented the question of bilaterality in an original and daring manner with the publication of *The Origin of Consciousness in the Breakdown of the Bicameral Mind*. Jaynes caused quite a stir at the time, offering a new explanation for the purpose of the two-sided, bicameral human brain (bicameral meaning two-chambered). The very idea that our mind is not a single, unified and monolithic entity--that it is in fact a two-chambered system--is somewhat unsettling. Jaynes built his theory about consciousness within the understanding that our mental environment is itself bicameral, a system that operates like a suite of two rooms joined by a common doorway. While Jaynes offers his unique theory in an attempt to explain the original purpose of the bicameral brain in humans, in the end, I was left to wrestle with the question for myself: *Just what is the purpose of our two-sided brain?*

Numerous developments in the science of mind subsequent to Jaynes' publication have supported the belief that the bilateral model of our body and mind is essentially accurate. Because the working details of this model are only beginning to be understood, we are forced to accommodate a less unified construct of the mind than we might wish to consider. The consequences of having a *second mind* to account for makes the task of understanding the brain not less but far more complex than it was before the two-sided structure of the mind was unveiled.

Current maps of our body and mind are in many ways just as crude as the maps of the physical world were six centuries ago. The belief that the earth was flat was fully supported by science, the church and society of the period. Just as flat earth views were abandoned when exposed to unsettling new truths, we too are faced with compelling new findings regarding the true nature of the body and mind. Roger Sperry's early work on split brain patients and subsequent findings made possible by modern scanning devices have opened windows into what was essentially a hidden system. As we explore this complex and mysterious inner world, we are busy setting aside the old maps, redefining and redrawing our maps of inner space.

In the flat-earth world view of Medieval times, if one sailed too close to the edge of the known world, currents would sweep them over the side and they would drop into the abyss. In my view, submergee training carries its victims over a different kind of edge, into an *internal abyss*. According to Stanley Coren's research, the journey over what one might refer to as the *submergee abyss* routinely takes place in children before the age of nine. The really interesting question for adults and particularly for submergee adults becomes, *What happens when one of these submergee children emerges as an adult?*

Since submergee and emergee experiences are linked to alterations in the interhemispheric boundaries of the brain and the connecting tissues of the corpus callosum, might we be able to learn something from research on the laterality of schizophrenic individuals? One area that the two groups may have in common is a violation of the normal boundaries or *operating rules* that the brain follows in coordinating functions between its hemispheres. One of many theories regarding schizophrenia considers the possibility that a faulty interhemispheric switching mechanism mediated by the corpus callosum may be a root cause of the condition. In normal humans, this switching mechanism governs a carefully coordinated interplay of processing between hemispheres. The research group studying this question in schizophrenics expressed their finding that these individuals appear to have a "sticky interhemispheric switch."[15]

While submergees certainly are not schizophrenics, research into abnormal brain function is commonly used by psychologists to shed light on related questions. The fact that the laterality of submergees is altered to accommodate reversed handedness raises a legitimate question about the impact of these alterations. If, as research indicates, a "sticky interhemispheric switch" may cause something as devastating as schizophrenia, alterations of the brain mechanisms that govern the laterality of submergees might also cause difficulties. Negative impacts on interhemispheric function that follow handedness reversals may explain losses in processing efficiency that have been observed in submergees, as well as other symptoms, such as a sense of alienation from self and others.

By studying subjects who could alter the normal collaboration between their two hemispheres, Andrew Newberg of the University of Pennsylvania, author of *Why God Won't Go Away*[16] touched upon the topic of alterations in interhemispheric coordination from a different perspective. Newberg and his colleagues highlighted the critical nature of hemispheric relationships, which are fundamental to our very sense of self. The work at University of Pennsylvania, which used brain scanning to study shifts in organizational patterns of subjects in states of deep meditation, demonstrated that collaboration between the two hemispheres is altered in significant ways by the practice.

While meditating, subjects in Newberg's research project reported a sense of becoming *one with the universe* stating that it was as if they were living in a world without boundaries. The study also raised the curtain on the mechanisms that enable us to maintain or revise the limits of our body and mind systems. Like the research findings on interhemispheric switching, Newberg's studies on meditation focused on the delicate interplay between consciousness and the supporting mechanisms of the brain which can be impacted when laterality is altered.

Many of the famous submergee leaders I have studied exhibit a version of the expansive point of view reported by Newberg's subjects when setting goals for the countries they govern. The unique rewiring of the brain created by abnormal and long-term pressures on the laterality of those who become submergees seems to in some sense mimic the loss of boundaries reported in Newburg's study. This peculiar submergee perspective is a trait that can have fascinating consequences when it governs the thinking and decisions made by an influential leader.

Consider the manner in which submergee President Ronald Reagan crossed over seemingly insuperable geo-political hurdles with his Star Wars program to confront the *Evil Empire* of the Soviet Union and put an end to the Cold War. Another submergee who has demonstrated this kind of really big thinking is Fidel Castro, whose influence assumed massive proportions during the Cuban missile crisis and later, in military interventions throughout the globe. Operating from an impoverished Caribbean island, Fidel continues to loom larger-than-life on the stage of Latin American politics and policy in the Western Hemisphere.

In my search for clues that would help me to understand questions pertaining to submergees and emergees, I have studied famous submergees and issues as diverse as the *handedness* of subatomic particles and the super-symmetry of the cosmos. At the very smallest to the largest scales, including the bilateral structures that make up our bodies and minds, our universe is a massive demonstration of coordinated or bilateral pairs. This principal of cooperating pairs forms the foundation of consciousness itself, a mysterious phenomenon which arises from a complex dance that takes place between two hemispheres and many individual sites in the body and mind.

We see the bilateral template in use in many categories, but in matters of consciousness, the question haunts us; *Why is the human nervous system physiologically bilateral, yet functionally asymmetrical?* Advances in science and access to massive resources of knowledge have in many ways made the puzzle a more detailed and difficult one to resolve. For me, the study of laterality in the body and mind has remained a personal fascination, because submergees and emergees travel across these boundaries.

LISTENING TO SUBMERGEES

A small number of submergee authors have written something about their experiences. One author who created a first-person account gives an autobiographical rendition of her experiences. The author is psychotherapist Eileen Simpson and the title of her book is *REVERSALS A Personal Account of Victory Over Dyslexia.* Those interested in gaining an additional first-hand account of a child's perspective on submergees should read Simpson's story. The book has significant value as a reference source because the author is a professionally trained observer. Simpson's narrative deals with events that took place before, during, and after the moment her first grade teacher converted her into a submergee. The story is told from the vantage point of a child and it is written with a careful eye for detail. Simpson's heart-breaking narrative shares the severe struggles and learning disabilities that followed her conversion experience.

Simpson shares a scene set in the classroom after the other students have all been excused for the day. The young student and her teacher, Mother Serafina, are alone.

Samuel M. Randolph

I relaxed my grip on the pen, let my fingers go limp. It was Mother Serafina who wrote the letter home, not I. But the possessor of the stronger hand also possessed the stronger will. By the end of the term I was as right-handed as all the other children. Or so it seemed.[17]

Interestingly, Simpson connects the switching incident above to her *dyslexia*, but she never decides to take the next step, to return to her native left-handedness. Perhaps she never considered emerging as a potential cure that should be given serious consideration. Why not? If Simpson had been privy to current research on laterality and plasticity, she might have developed a better understanding of the nature of her trauma and then chosen to emerge from the walls of the right-handed prison she portrays vividly in her book.

Simpson's story is ultimately one of succeeding in spite of her handicaps. The real question which is raised by her book is, *What steps should submergees take if they become aware that a handedness reversal is the root cause of their problems?* An equally important question that we all must answer is, *How shall we put an end to this problem altogether?*

Jack Fincher, another submergee author, spoke up in *Lefties - The Origins & Consequences Of Being Left-Handed* written in 1977.

Looking back at my own indoctrination into a dominantly right-handed world, [I had to ask myself] was I permanently, devastatingly, secretly damaged? I think--at least I hope--not. As a practicing left-hander, I simply and silently went underground. Or, in the negative sense of today's vernacular, into the closet. I learned to write and sharpen pencils with my right hand passably, and to draw with real skill. My transformation, though, was not without a subtle slippage in spatial orientation. Handedness, we are beginning to suspect, may be more a matter of sidedness--of hand, foot, eye, and body, both inside and out, though much of the evidence remains murky.[18]

Thirty years after Fincher wrote these words regarding handedness and the related issue of sidedness (his way of referring to laterality) the evidence is far less murky.

Another submergee author whom I discovered just in time to help with the writing of this book is Bernard Selling, author of *Writing from Within: A Guide to Creativity and Life Story Writing*. I was blessed by Selling's wonderful book, but imagine my surprise when Selling confessed in his book that he was a deep submergee! He wrote that, like me, he discovered that he had been trained to become right-handed without retaining memories of the experience.

For a long time, I tried writing creatively, but without much success. Then along came the computer. At the keyboard I could type with both hands, correcting and moving things around almost as quickly as I could think.

Sometime after that my sister asked, "Did you know that you were left-handed as a child?" *I reacted with surprise.* "Dad didn't think it would be good for you to be left-handed," *she continued,* "so he had you changed."[19]

As illustrated by the words of these three authors, those who go looking for information about submergees can find it if they look patiently and carefully. Our biased perspectives and culturally established mind-sets selectively blind us. We cannot see or know that submergees live everywhere in our world until we first understand and accept the fact that they can and do exist.

I would like to recognize three additional authors, men who have labored to overcome cultural bias and blindness as they have written about issues that relate directly or indirectly to submergees and emergees. The first is Professor Stanley Coren of the University of British Columbia at Vancouver. Coren writes about the problems of bias and blindness relating to handedness in *The Left-Hander Syndrome: The Causes And Consequences Of Left-Handedness*. Coren is one of only a few who have conducted surveys and collected data that illustrates our blindness to matters of handedness. Professor Coren's review and reporting of the data available on handedness reversals includes consideration of the high incidence of the practice in certain Asian populations, which he documents in this book. The book stands alone as an excellent research source for the study and understanding of the unique issues that affect submergees. Coren's pithy insights into many seldom-discussed issues related to handedness help to make *The Left-Hander Syndrome* a meaningful work.

A second champion, who has developed a reputation for his unique manner of reporting on the internal states of others, is renowned author and neurologist, Oliver Sacks, MD. Sack's clear and compassionate observations based on unusual shifts in human perception and experience are masterpieces. As explained near the beginning of this chapter, Sacks also provided me with the strong encouragement I needed to write this book.

In his autobiography, *A Leg To Stand On*, which was written in 1984, Sacks describes his encounter with anosognoisia, the loss and subsequent recovery of his brain's awareness of his damaged leg. The observations that Sacks shares about his disconnection and re-connection to his leg helped me develop a deeper understanding of the mechanisms which are at work on a larger scale in submergees. In 1993, Sacks returned to his autobiography with an after word. The after word takes up the topic of anosognoisia with fresh insights, including the biological basis for primary consciousness and "a neurology of identity" as well as related issues such as large-scale plasticity and adaptation in adults as a thoughtful supplement to the original narrative. The book has relevance for those who would like to gain a meaningful perspective on events of alienation and homecoming that can and do occur in the body and mind.

Author John Ritter, whom I mentioned in chapter two, has written an excellent novel, *Choosing Up Sides*. This book gives readers a fictional first-hand account of a submergee boy who decides to play baseball as a left-handed pitcher against his father's wishes. The father is a preacher who views the left hand as an instrument of the devil. Because the boy has a natural gift for pitching, he finds himself caught in a real predicament — or "pickle," — to use baseball terms.

116

Choosing Up Sides is an easy-to-read and dramatic example of the struggle to be left-handed in a cultural setting where expressions of left-handedness were strongly discouraged. The book is written for children, but it is also a wonderful resource for adult readers who are interested in learning more about how children's preferred handedness can be subjected to intense social pressure. As the story reaches its climax, the protagonist has a chance to watch Babe Ruth play in a charity baseball game. The Babe, who began playing baseball as a left-handed pitcher, was switched to the outfield so he could bat more often. Babe Ruth had more than his position on the baseball field switched. In real life, the Babe was a submergee.

SUBMERGEES UNDER THE MICROSCOPE ~ CHAPTER 11

Dear Abby: I am the mother of a baby who is learning to feed himself. I am almost positive that Terry is left-handed, because when I put the spoon in his right hand, he transfers it to his left and proceeds eating that way.

My husband says I should train Terry to be right-handed, because everything is geared for right-handed people and the boy will be handicapped if he's left-handed. Now my husband is forcing Terry to eat with his right hand.

What do your experts say?

Young Mother[20]

THE LEFT-HANDED MICROSCOPE

I pity Abby and anyone else who is asked to act as an expert who can respond confidently to questions about the do's and don'ts of handedness in young children. In the absence of qualified sources of information, mothers and other adults who could use expert advice relating to the development of handedness are commonly offered biased and contradictory opinions. Society would benefit greatly from an accurate and scientifically-based presentation of what is wise and what is foolish.

As soon as I was able to gain my own sense of what the left-handed world was really like, it wasn't long before I realized that the world of the lefty into which I had been born wasn't what I had thought it would be. Use of items as familiar and simple as the controls on a microscope now seemed alien, because it was presupposed that the user would be right-handed!

Hidden Handedness

Observations of the right-handed world, such as my encounter with the microscope and a host of other tools and manufactured objects that were designed for right-handers, initiated a lefty learning process in me. I slowly began to understand what it meant to be a member of a minority group: those who are left-handed. Professor Stanley Coren outlined some of the environmental dynamics that are a factor for left-handed individuals.

Right-handers might feel that words such as 'discrimination' used with reference to left-handers are a bit overdone or melodramatic. I (as a right-hander) certainly would have felt that way when I began researching the psychology and neuropsychology of handedness some twenty years ago. But through that research it became clear to me that most of us do have a set of often-unacknowledged attitudes toward left-handers that express themselves in condescension and even scorn.

Coren also notes that this minority group . . . *constitutes about 10 percent of the present human population. Like many other minority groups it has been subject to prejudice, humiliation, and discrimination-- not on the basis of race, religion, age or national origin, but simply on the basis of the hand that its members use for such everyday acts as brushing teeth or cutting food.*[21]

The Internet provides us with ready access to information about minority viewpoints, and since left-handers fit into this category, an Internet search on left-handedness will provide ample insight into the issues on which Coren and many others have reported.

But I had another question to address: what can be known about the inner world of submergees? What were their unique experiences like? Once I began to understand something of the history and experiences of the left-handed minority, the world of the submergee minority began to open up too. I was greatly surprised to discover that a few of my friends and acquaintances were actually submergees! With great curiosity, I began to interview these first submergee volunteers and I began to learn what I needed to know by listening to them tell their own stories about handedness.

The life experiences of submergees brought into view the first outlines of a bigger and more complete picture of this special people group. The first submergee I became acquainted with in this manner was my own father. He found my decision to become an emergee rather fascinating and humorous. Both of us are still somewhat amused by the strange turn of events that my emergee discovery initiated, especially since the learning process I have been through is an experience that I have been able to share with him on a daily basis. The one common element shared by all of the submergees I have interviewed is the rather tantalizing knowledge that we are discussing a subject that no one has ever brought up before, that our life-experiences don't exist on society's radar screen.

Thanks to these early submergee interviews, I gained enough understanding of the life-experiences of submergees to begin asking more focused questions. Knowing the right questions to ask made the interview process much more effective. An example of a positive interview response that helped me to know that I was speaking to a submergee would be a case where an individual shared intact memories of switching (a normal submergee).

It has been surprising to learn that a large number of submergees are prepared to give detailed reports of their submergee training experiences at the hands of adults. Identifying those who do not have memories of the switching experience (deep submergees) is an entirely different matter, since there are no standardized procedures and protocols for this purpose.

As a more detailed picture of submergees began to emerge, I encountered a fact that I hadn't expected. I learned that the population of submergees-in-hiding was far larger than I had expected it would be. Keep in mind that in my first attempts at forming an understanding of submergees, I had thought that the percentages of people who would fit into this category had to be extremely small. In my mind it seemed reasonable to assume that perhaps one half of one percent or less of the world's population might be submergees.

While I was pleased to connect with others who had developmental experiences and struggles like mine, the obvious implication was that the population of submergees was far higher than I had thought it was. Although the sample of people I was able to access and interview represented a very small numeric base, I realized that there was a distinct possibility that the small percentages I had been projecting for the world's submergee population had been overly conservative.

My research now shifted from a completely personal story about an unknown subject that was of interest to me alone, into names and faces that I knew and could learn from. Once that *externalization* of the submergee story happened, I began to see my history in much better detail. I was able to empathize with and understand others who had become submergees because of social pressure or a desire to conform to the norms of the right-handed majority.

In an interesting exception to the practice of conforming to the right-handed norm, my interviews also revealed another group of submergees: right-handed children born to parents who preferred to have left-handed offspring. Although these children who have been trained to become left-handed submergees are not as common as left-handed children trained to be right-handed submergees, the training process appears to work in both directions. Adults can and do submerge left-handed children by turning them into fake rightys and they also can and do submerge right-handed children, turning them into fake leftys.

With the finding that a significant segment of the world's population suffers from submergee deficits, my eyes were opened to the fact that the submergee problem is a serious social concern. Discovering something of the scale of the problem gave me one of my first major incentives to bring the submergee story into the public square.

The two stories which follow are drawn from real experiences I had during my first years as an emergee when I was wondering if I should or shouldn't share my story with others. Both happen to be set in the context of business travel and as such, they will give a sense of what my experiences were like as a newly minted emergee.

THE BLIND LEADING THE BLIND

I am seated between two passengers on a flight from Los Angeles to New Orleans. As usual, I am busy with research work on handedness and laterality. It's been a little more than a year and a month since I emerged. The research project I am engaged in is part of a crash course aimed at discovering what happened to me when I became left-handed. The material I am reading is absolutely fascinating and I am absorbed in marking up the reports and articles.

As our meals are served, I note that the young man seated next to the window on my left is eating using his left hand to hold his fork. He is wearing his watch on his right wrist so I ask him *Are you left-handed?* He affirms my guess and we share a few thoughts on the topic.

His name is Kevin. He is a landscape architect, living in Los Angeles and returning home to visit his family in New Orleans. Kevin says he loves his work, and at age twenty-six he appears to have a very bright future.

At this point in my research project, I've become rather alarmed by the surprisingly large number of cases in which prejudice against left-handed individuals is reported on the various websites I've been visiting, so I decide to check my findings with Kevin.

Kevin, what was it like for you to grow up as a lefty? Did you experience any attempts to switch your handedness, any sense of shame or any sense that you needed to conform to the right-handed world's expectations? To my surprise, Kevin flatly denies that he has ever had the slightest struggle or even a hint that *those kinds of problems* still exist in the modern world that he has known. His personal experiences totally contradict my findings.

But Kevin, I protest, *not only are there numerous books written on this subject, but there is a ton of information on the Internet that documents the experiences of left-handed people all around the world who are still treated as members of an undesirable minority. Haven't you ever visited any of the left-handed websites?*

No.

I decide to change the subject. *So,* I ask, *what's going on in New Orleans, Kevin?*

Kevin says, *Well, my father, step-mother and younger brother live in the city and I'm taking the week off to catch up with my family. With my work schedule, this is a really important break for me. One thing upsets me though: my step-mom has been forcing my nine year old left-handed brother to be right-handed. She's really something else.*

I'm eager to get back to my reading, so after wishing Kevin a great vacation, I return to my work for another 90 minutes. I'm grateful to have time to read and mark up my research articles until we land and leave the plane. The incredible irony of our conversation totally escapes me at the time.

This true story (or might I say comedy?) illustrates a critical fact of life: new ways of looking at ourselves and at others most often have to develop gradually. This is especially true when the beliefs and precepts that have to change come pre-packaged in a culturally sanctioned bias such as those we hold towards handedness. As I learned in my visit with Kevin, the views of others regarding handedness are difficult to challenge, and my own views on handedness were also slow to change. In my case, three years passed before I returned to review my notes of our visit and I finally caught on to the ironic moment in our conversation when Kevin directly contradicted himself.

Had I expected to encounter Kevin's self-inflicted contradiction in the course of our short visit, I could have easily "caught" him in his own words and shown him just how far out of sync his assumptions really were. But even with an illustration as powerful as the one he unwittingly provided, I doubt that Kevin would have been prepared to change his thinking on the spot. One of the statements Kevin made in dismissing the possibility that a problem such as discrimination against left-handed people existed was his certainty that *nothing like that happens in America anymore, that's something that happened fifty years ago, but it certainly isn't a problem now.*

While it's easy to criticize Kevin for his blindness to the issues his left-handed brethren face, we all suffer from bias and preconceived notions of the world we live in. Did you notice how long it took for me to catch on to the humorous moment that was tucked away and hidden within our conversation?

Tales From The Crypt

Two years after my visit with Kevin, I am returning from another business trip and headed for California on a wide body jet. I am seated in the center of three seats that are located adjacent to the outside of the aircraft. Our seats open to an emergency exit and my row faces forward while the passengers in front of us face backward creating a conversational space for six. Amy, our flight attendant is a tall, beautiful African-American woman. She takes her seat opposite mine and is facing me as the plane lifts off. After we are airborne, she begins the in-flight passenger service and as she passes near our group, she overhears me talking casually about handedness issues with one of the passengers in our group. As soon as Amy returns to her seat, she catches my eye and confesses that she overheard our conversation and is keenly interested in hearing more of my story now that she can relax.

Would you be willing to share your story with the rest of us? Amy says.

With the encouragement of everyone in our group, I begin to explain what it was like to emerge into my native left-handed state after forty years of being submerged and living as a right-handed person. To my intense pleasure, I find that, after more than three frustrating years of struggling to verbalize this experience to strangers, I am able to tell my story quickly, summarizing the important details with ease, and doing so in a way that makes sense to everyone.

All of us are having a wonderful time. I am comforted and encouraged by the surprising warmth and acceptance I can sense from each listener. Every member of our group has something to share about concerns related to handedness. Even if they aren't connected to the topic directly, everyone is either related to or close friends with a person whose life has been affected by the issues that concern me. To my amazement, one by one, all of them join in, making their own contributions. Everyone in the group is eager to share the story of how their life has been touched. I am doubly amazed, first at the way the story hits home with all five members of the group, and second, with the way everyone can so easily connect with my story and then move on to share their own insights and experiences.

After listening to what the others have to say, Amy confesses that she has a special reason for asking to hear my story. With a tone that's more serious than I expected, she tells us her family's story.

I grew up in a family of nine children. Of those nine, seven of us were born left-handed. I guess you could say I was one of the two lucky ones, because I was born right-handed. One by one, as each of my brothers and sisters grew older, my mom and dad would watch them to see if they were going to be left-handed. Of those seven out of nine who were left-handed, every one had to learn to become right-handed.

Now that we have all grown up, every one of my brothers and sisters who were switched had some form of a serious struggle or problem in their life, first in school and later as adults. One of my brothers has struggled for years with drugs, depression and suicidal tendencies. None of those that were switched have had anything like the quality of life that I have had. Where I succeeded in school and on the job without a struggle, they have always had serious problems. I know that what you are talking about is a serious issue, but I have never heard anybody explain the kind of problems that switching causes. So far as I know, nobody has ever talked to any of my bothers or sisters who were switched about the source of their problems, or the possibility of just becoming left-handed again.

125

Amazed by Amy's story, I promise her and the others in our group that I will get on with writing my story for publication ASAP. I can see clearly that my horror story pales in comparison to the one Amy has just shared. I am numbed by the impact of her family history. She had not one or two, but <u>seven</u> seriously traumatized submergee siblings, whose lives were permanently damaged by their unfortunate experience.

In spite of the incentive and encouragement I received from friends and acquaintances who advised that I "just had to go public and tell the story" *eight more years* would pass before the struggle to write this book was complete. In spite of my intense motivation to finish the work, I believe it was a saving grace that my story remained under wraps, until I had time to see the full scope of the emergee experience. I also needed time to come to grips with the struggle of privacy issues and, equally important, time to develop my writing skills.

I realized that I was in no way prepared to present the issue of submergees or emergees from the vantage point of an expert. I remained convinced for the first three years after emerging that the experts would became acquainted with my story and then they would pick up on the critical importance of the submergee issue and make it their own cause. During those first few years I thought, *Aren't we an educated, information rich, curious and talkative society and isn't the Internet there to inform everyone about new or unusual developments exactly like this one?*

Instead of becoming a topic that the experts wanted to study and discuss, the story of submergees and emergees languished and the years passed with no interest shown and no action taken. I became increasingly frustrated as I began to realize that no experts were going to surface to take up the cause and share the submergee story with the world. The silence I encountered in my first four years of searching for help was eerie. Then something truly bizarre happened. After fourteen years of research, a biographer named Edmund Morris published the authorized biography *Dutch: A Memoir of Ronald Reagan.*

THE DUTCH DOOR OPENS ~ CHAPTER 12

They say the world has become too complex for simple answers. They are wrong. There are no easy answers, but there are simple answers. We must have the courage to do what we know is morally right. Winston Churchill said that "The destiny of man is not measured by material computation. When great forces are on the move in the world, we learn we are spirits -- not animals." And he said, "There is something going on in time and space, and beyond time and space, which, whether we like it or not, spells duty."

Address to the nation, October 27, 1964 - Ronald Reagan

I was vacationing on the Oregon coast in October of 1999 when a massive media storm broke with the publication of *Dutch: A Memoir of President Ronald Reagan* by Edmund Morris. The controversy created by the publication of *Dutch* centered on the rather bizarre treatment accorded President Reagan by his authorized biographer. In an interview with Newsweek Magazine published at the height of the storm's fury, Morris himself referred to his work as "a strange book about a strange man." Because Morris had earned a Pulitzer Prize for his biography of President Teddy Roosevelt, the fact that President Reagan had been treated in such an unusual manner by Morris caused quite a stir. Some of the comments that appeared in print follow:

(Ronald Reagan's) extremely peculiar nature is back in the news, thanks to the release this Thursday of one of the most eagerly anticipated tomes in American political history, **Dutch: A Memoir of Ronald Reagan,** *by Edmund Morris. . . for 14 years he toiled on the project . . . That experience has apparently driven Mr. Morris batty.*

Edward Achchorn in *The Providence Journal Bulletin*. Reported in USA Today 10/1/99 in the Opinion Line column.

Samuel M. Randolph

A San Francisco Chronicle article dated 10/14/99 stated that

. . . reactions have ranged from delight to outrage. Ron Reagan Jr. appeared on "60 minutes" to praise the book's emotional veracity, while New York Times book critic Michiko Kakutani denounced it as "bizarre, irresponsible and monstrously self-absorbed." Columnist George Will called "Dutch" a "dishonorable" work. Columnist Maureen Dowd simply declared Morris "barking mad."

In the Bay Area on a promotional tour, the South African born Morris, 59, looks surprisingly chipper for a man who has unleashed the biggest literary storm since "Ulysses" got nailed on obscenity charges . . . But Reagan proved as elusive as his character's amputated legs in his most acclaimed film "Kings Row." And eventually, after years of interviews laced with aimless anecdotes and oblique answers, Morris was left to echo that film's most famous line: "Where's the rest of him?" . . .

Article by Neva Chonin, San Francisco Chronicle 10/14/99

The fear is that crazy Edmund has the story--has found a way to tell this unbelievable tale. The reality distortion that dare not speak its name. This fear is not unwarranted. There is something in the nature of the book, its weirdness, its extremes, that makes you realize--more than a well-mannered detailing of the archival evidence might--how truly bizarre the Reagan years were. Fictional bizarre. Comedy bizarre. Bizarre bizarre. Inevitably you get to thinking, there must have been a conspiracy to create normality here--a conspiracy between the press and the Reaganites, a cabal of silence (although with much snickering as great as when the press hid the Kennedy scandals). Or greater. Much greater. This man was strange. Profoundly weird. Not just disconnected but gone.

Michael Wolff article *Dutch Treat*, NY Times Book Review 10/10/99.

But does Dutch *finally penetrate the mystery of RR, explain the calculated spontaneity, the cold warmth, the absent presence? No, yet in passage after passage it captures the paradoxes that make up the man.*

Hidden Handedness

Christopher Lehmann-Haupt, NY Times News Service 10/3/99.

Biographers say they have to guard against taking on the characteristics of their subjects. But Morris has surrendered completely. He has himself become a creature of Reaganesque unreality.

Maureen Dowd, NY Times Service 9/23/99.

On the side of moral and intellectual relativism and, possibly, genuine flakiness, is Edmund Morris, the frail-looking biographer.

Michael Wolff, New York 10/18/99.

For certain, future biographies--and less "creative" ones--will be needed to fill in the crater sized holes of this American life. But Dutch never fails to evoke the power and mystery of its subject. "Where's the rest of me?" indeed.

Steven R. Weisman *The Hollow Man* The New York Times Book Review 10/10/99.

What a shame it is that, after 14 years of research and writing, Edmund Morris had to resort to fiction to tell us what he thinks Ronald Reagan was all about. . . . Unable to get the president to "open up" for him, Morris decided to open Reagan up through the use of fictional characters to whom Morris would give the job of analyzing the president. It doesn't seem to have worked very well.

Lyn Nofziger 10/1/99 USA Today

In a move of unprecedented weirdness, the Pulitzer Prize winning Morris . . . has created an imaginary friend, also named Edmund Morris, who begins to shadow Reagan in the mid-1920's and serves as the book's narrator - until the late 1960's, when the fictional biographer morphs into Morris himself . . . Reading James Joyce while skateboarding through rush-hour traffic would have been a less arduous task . . . I was prepared to give Morris the benefit of the doubt. This biography, though, is something completely different--a work so bizarre and byzantine, so utterly frustrating in its trickery and its madness, that it's not a biography at all--it's a hallucination, a bad trip, a wrong way crash through the looking glass and into a parallel and quite phony past.

Chicago Sun-Times: Richard Roeper Reported in USA Today 10/1/99 in the Opinion line column.

. . . Perhaps Morris made up a fictional character to take the blame for calling Reagan 'an apparent air head.' Or maybe Morris just needed more than 14 years to think about history. Whatever the reason, the effort doesn't seem worthy of a respected writer and does not add any perspective to history or the profound impact Reagan has had on it.

Daily News, Los Angeles, in an editorial. Reported in USA Today 10/1/99 in the Opinion line column.

Random House, the publisher of *Dutch* must have been concerned about the poor reception that readers might give to this unusual book, because they mention the unusual nature of the work in a comment which appears on the book's flap.

. . . Morris' biographical mind becomes in effect another character in the narrative . . .

When Morris was asked "What do you really think of Ronald Reagan?" he responded:

I have gradually, over the course of many years, come to the conclusion that he was a great president. More interesting to me than greatness however, is that he was throughout his life such a strange combination of innocence and wisdom, charm and hard force, gregariousness and aloofness, egocentricity without conceit, aggression without cruelty, imaginativeness and cultural ignorance, sentimentality and emotional coolness. I could go on for a quarter of an hour and not exhaust his contrary opposites. He is also--to finish with a simple statement--the bravest and most incorrupt figure I've ever studied.

Newsweek 10/4/1999.

Since I was on vacation when the scandal hit and had the luxury of plenty of free time, I was able to track the details of this storm as it struck and then spent its fury. The charges and countercharges, attacks and defenses flew about over the airwaves and in print. What a stir this book had managed to make!

Because of my prior research on submergees, I already knew that President Reagan was left-handed. I also knew that his father was an alcoholic. Could *Dutch* become the door of understanding I needed in order to offer readers a detailed example of a submergee that could be used to introduce others to the subject? My journal notes for October 1, 1999 read:

The news of President Reagan comes as a real thought provoker. Was he a submergee as I seem to recall? Is my information correct? Question number one: is he a submergee?

Filled with hope that I might have found an example of a submergee who was also a prominent public figure, I called the nearest bookstore and learned that two copies of *Dutch* were still on their shelves. The clerk agreed to hold a copy for me and thirty minutes later I had purchased my prize, a biography of six hundred and seventy-four pages including the epilogue and poems by Morris.

Returning from the bookstore, I dove into the pages of this rather bewildering book. In my excitement, I overlooked the rather bizarre manner of the biography as I worked to learn something new from the account. My search was quickly rewarded.

Morris spoke, in what seemed to me to be a whispered confidence, of locating the evidence of Ronald Reagan's early handwriting samples. The discovery took place as a happy accident, while he was doing research at the archives of the Ronald Reagan Presidential Library. The crucial evidence was discovered in a tin that contained early letters handwritten by the President. These letters were the clue that could unravel the mystery of the inner Ronald Reagan.

Morris' instincts for accurate reporting hit the mark perfectly. He found three examples of Ronald Reagan's handwriting, portions of which are reproduced in *Dutch*. The examples of Reagan's handwriting were completed at ages fourteen, sixteen and seventeen. These samples appear on page ninety three of the biography in concert with Morris' statements that:

Only the occasional involuntary straightening of an I shows that the penman is forcing himself to write with his right hand which is what Midwestern orthodoxy required of southpaw schoolboys in the mid 1920's. The script becomes more shapely after the acquisition of a fountain pen in 1927.[22]

By the summer of 1928 however, Mr. Reagan's left-handed undertow begins to hoist the masts of his perpendiculars upright, like a canvas anchor drifting contrary to the wind.[23]

Morris uses a pair of metaphors that are pregnant with insight when he refers to the "left-handed undertow" and "contrary drifting anchor" in Reagan's penmanship. He accurately reports his sense of the contrary currents and struggles that exist within submergees such as Reagan.

Yes I thought, *Edmund Morris, you were looking at the key to the Dutch door of President Reagan's body and mind the moment that you found those hidden letters and read them. You intuitively knew they were important. But where could you turn for further insight into their meaning? What effect did President Reagan's submergee experience actually have on him? The full meaning of these clues and the critical role that your subject's submergee state played in shaping his life, his thoughts and behavior eluded you. In unearthing the evidence of his submergee soul, you had observed something that couldn't be understood at the time, because submergees didn't have an identity, they didn't exist.*

In his footnote to page 93 Morris cites a diary entry of John Hutton referencing President Reagan and dated August 27, 1987:

As long as he could remember things seemed more natural with his left hand, but by convention he had learned to use his right. His dominant eye was his left.[24]

Morris continues with his own note on the topic of handedness:

Other signs of RR's suppressed left-handedness: as an actor he shot and twirled his revolver in his left hand, and slapped and punched with it. He combed his hair from right to left and when accosted by photographers, always tended to wave with his left hand. Of all the forty presidential signatures reproduced in the anteroom of the Reagan Library Museum, RR's is the only one that slopes backward.[25]

Morris cites a long list of strange characteristics of the President in *Dutch*, all of which are documented in detail. A few of the examples which I found especially interesting are:

His phonographic memory (pg. 117-118) and his photographic memory (pg. 626-627). The sense of a strange shrinking and reappearance phenomena or shift that was observed by Morris as Reagan prepared to speak to live cameras in the televised speech given at the end of his presidency (pg. 647-649). Complaints by staffers that they had to remind Governor Reagan who they were every time he saw them (pg. 394).[26]

The fact that Morris captured President Reagan in the lucid manner that he did validates his statement made to Neva Chonin of the San Francisco Chronicle *I like to represent the strangeness of life*, he adds. *The real things. When real things are looked at properly, they're usually very strange.* Article by Neva Chonin San Francisco Chronicle 10/14/99

An example of the keen eye of Morris for the subject of his study can be seen in the selection of the cover photograph for *Dutch*. The cover photo is a black and white picture of the President, shot from behind. The photo was taken as he waved to White House staff, with his left hand. Reagan's right side and hand are in shadow, while his left hand and the left side of his body are highlighted in a sunny framework. The irony of this multi-layered, mirror view of President Reagan signaling with his left hand is one of many examples where Morris, or others he worked with in creating *Dutch*, successfully represented the President's strangeness.

Morris' work proved to be a timely godsend that gave my writing project a much-needed boost. At the same time, I really felt sorry for him because I sensed that his experience in writing *Dutch* must have been something like assuming the role of Captain Ahab in *Moby Dick* as he undertook the quest of mastering the mysterious and elusive great white whale. In reading *Dutch* and following Morris in his interviews subsequent to publication, it became clear that the work of understanding and conveying the inner nature of the President was a struggle which went far beyond anything he had expected to encounter. Like a modern-day Captain Ahab, Morris tenaciously sought to capture his prey in the pages of a biography, but instead he was pulled underwater by the mysterious undertow of President Reagan. As Maureen Dowd put it in speaking of Morris, "He [Morris] has become a creature of Reaganesque unreality."

If we recognize the fact that *Dutch* represents a sincere attempt to portray the inner essence of a submergee subject, Morris has to be given credit as a literary pioneer who paid the price to do what had to be done. In a sense, Morris became a "submergee biographer" in order to write about President Reagan by creating a fictional self in the pages of *Dutch*. This device was adopted in spite of the fact that readers found it very difficult to accept.

In Morris' words:

I quite understand that readers will have to adjust, at first, to what amounts to a new biographical style. But the revelations of this style, which derive directly from Ronald Reagan's own way of looking at his life, are I think rewarding enough to convince them that one of the most interesting characters in recent American history looms here like a colossus.[27]

Given his subject, Morris' style is apt, but the technique, which was developed as a means to communicate the submergee reality that Morris encountered, exposes readers to a dizzying world of reality mixed with fiction. In short, Morris had to find a way to take us through the looking glass of the submergee body and mind in order to portray the real person he was writing about.

In my view, *Dutch* exhibits Morris' genius as a biographer. Were it not for his persistence and most of all, his refusal to be intimidated by the strange nature of his study, we would have been deprived of this wonderful opportunity to gaze into the soul of a man whom Americans knew well but understand poorly. The enigma of the President would have stopped a lesser man in his tracks. Morris will eventually be given his due, and appreciated as a very brave writer who did what he had to do in order to truthfully report what he observed.

From my vantage point as an emergee, the most important outcome of Morris' "barking madness" was the fact that it was now possible to refer to a public submergee whose nature had been faithfully portrayed by a biographer. Morris had managed to bring the special strangeness of President Reagan to the surface for inspection by faithfully revealing this unique man to his readers. Anyone who reads *Dutch* is reading an intimate biography about a man who has been positively identified as a submergee, in a manner that opens the subject up for inspection.

Finding and reading *Dutch* was a critical development for me, because it provided me with the kind of third-party evidence I urgently needed in order to illustrate the unique characteristics of submergees. The book also had therapeutic value, because I saw many elements of my own character portrayed in Reagan's life. As I read about President Reagan the submergee, I realized that I was also learning new things about myself.

An insight into the level of *hemispheric suppression,* or the functional penalty that the President paid in order to operate as a submergee, comes from the numerous reports of his inability to put a name with a face. This difficulty was just one of many bizarre quirks of Ronald Reagan. In one of the more glaring illustrations of the problem, Reagan failed to recognize his own son Michael while acting as guest of honor and speaker at his son's high school graduation. Approaching Michael, Reagan looked right into his son's face and greeted him with the statement "Hi, my name's Ronald Reagan. What's yours?"[28]

The price President Reagan paid for his submergee function might be thought of as a form of a *neurological override*. Alternately, one could think of his inability to put names together with faces as a *neurological traffic jam*, one that made the relatively complex process of interhemispheric association slower than average, if not impossible, for the President. As a submergee, he had to override his innate laterality for handedness and this *neurological override* played havoc in instances where intense and accurate interhemispheric sharing is required (e.g. putting a name with a face).

Some who are familiar with President Reagan's history have pointed out that his submergee deficits and odd behaviors may have resulted from a medical condition, from early manifestations of his Alzheimer's disease. The President was diagnosed with and did suffer from degenerative cognitive dementia. However, the value of the Reagan story arose from its relevance to others as a unique character study of a prominent figure, one that illustrates a submergee persona in action. So in spite of the fact that Reagan's history was clouded by Alzheimer's disease, the detailed record we have of this submergee's behavior, his special quirks that were in place from his early years, makes his story important. The fact that the unique submergee characteristics seen in Reagan's earlier years persisted until disease and then death ended his story makes it highly probable that the Reagan history we have is one that was unclouded by Alzheimer's until the very end, following trauma suffered in a riding accident in July of 1989. The riding accident occurred after Reagan's second term had ended, but not during the critical years that form the bulk of his life story

The decline in function, which was significant enough to be observed and reported by Morris and others, followed the incident in July 1989. This history raises the possibility that the brains of submergees may be abnormally vulnerable to damage from concussions due to their unique configuration. A striking parallel to Reagan's history exists in the history of submergee President Harry Truman. Many years after retirement, Truman, who was still vital and active at the time, fell in his bathroom and suffered a serious concussion. Subsequent to the concussion, biographers reported a serious decline in Truman's functional capacities.

Were President Reagan's strange submergee behaviors simply early manifestations of his Alzheimer's disease? Since his was a degenerative disease, the fact that Reagan's many unusual behaviors were already in place from his earliest years (a history that was carefully catalogued by Morris) does not support that line of reasoning. The record shows that Reagan served two terms as President, taking office at age sixty-nine, when many of his contemporaries had already retired. President Reagan stepped down eight years later at age seventy-seven. On balance, I would argue that Reagan's life history presents us with a rare and very meaningful doorway into the world of a bona fide submergee.

Once one understands that President Reagan was a submergee, the many comments from writers who plainly reported their perception that he was "bizarre" all make perfect sense. Keep in mind the fact that many of those who have written about Reagan's unusual and puzzling behaviors were speaking of something they had observed first-hand. The president's unique submergee behaviors would also explain the instincts of Nancy Reagan and others surrounding the President who carefully protected him from circumstances where his submergee character might be exposed in a manner that would create unfavorable images in the mind of the public. In order to protect against unflattering publicity, images of the Reagan White House were skillfully filtered. When in office, the President's words and deeds were managed by one of the most sophisticated presidential image control and PR teams ever assembled for this purpose.

In *For the Record*, Donald Regan writes,

He [Michael Deaver] saw — designed--each Presidential action as a one-minute or two-minute spot on the evening network news, or a picture on page one of the Washington Post or the New York Times, and conceived every Presidential appearance in terms of camera angles . . . His position was always chosen with the idea of keeping him as far away as possible from the reporters who hovered at the edge of these events with the intention of shouting questions. Every moment of every public appearance was scheduled, every word was scripted, every place where Reagan was expected to stand was chalked with toe marks.[29]

As a submergee, Reagan had difficulty functioning in situations where he needed to utilize rapid and complex mental processing that depended upon high-order exchanges of information between both hemispheres. In order to accommodate the functional deficits created by his submergee wiring, Reagan learned at a young age to use his excellent memory in order to overcome his submergee limitations. An example of this kind of challenge would be telling spontaneous jokes. In *Dutch,* Morris notes that Reagan was famous for drawing endlessly upon his large repertoire of canned jokes and humorous anecdotes which he had learned by studying comedians until he could precisely imitate their timing and delivery in his endless comedic replays.

Reagan's use of memorized humor enabled him to compensate for his limited ability to actually be funny spontaneously. Ironically, had he not exhibited the unique behaviors that are associated with submergees, many of the special talents that made Reagan a great leader, such as his inexhaustible store of canned humor, would not have been needed. Rather than being an example of an Alzheimer's induced degenerative disability, Reagan's strange brand of humor demonstrates a coping mechanism for the kind of unique functional constraints that submergees must overcome.

Once I had read *Dutch,* my fears of being unable to tell the submergee story publicly were put to rest. *Yes,* I thought gratefully *this book is the touchstone I had to find in order to connect submergees to the larger world they live in.* The so-called madness of Morris which enabled him to capture his submergee subject so clearly in *Dutch* provided me with a realistic portrait of a submergee character with whom others could identify. In the process of reading *Dutch,* those who complained about Morris' writing had been exposed first-hand to an intimate portrayal of a famous submergee. Thanks to "Crazy Edmund" I had the key I needed to open a door into the world of submergees that others could enter.

The thrill of finally meeting a fellow submergee up close in the pages of *Dutch* was an exciting experience. Not only did I become acquainted with this important President, but I also found myself looking at many of my own unique quirks as they were illustrated in his life. Having had the unpleasant experience of being called "weird" many times at various moments in my life, it was comforting to recognize myself in many of the puzzled references to Reagan that were recorded by Morris. Copious use of adjectives like "bizarre" and "strange" coming from those who wrote about Reagan's mysterious inner workings didn't surprise me in the least because these were adjectives that had once been applied to me.

THE OTHER SIDE OF THE DUTCH DOOR

As soon as I finished *Dutch* I developed a desire to discover more examples of famous submergees. I refer to this period in my life as the beginning of my "Biographical Period," a time of intense research into the lives of famous submergees that lasted for more than two years. I had struck gold in *Dutch* and I was eager to find if other lodes of precious insights existed in published works.

The downside of this biographical treasure hunt was the huge blocks of time that it consumed. Because biographies of famous subjects who are or were submergees are not written with that fact in mind, time-saving tools such as indexes and reference sources regarding submergees don't exist. Researching and building resources regarding historical submergee figures could easily become a rewarding field to pursue for those with an interest in this unexplored avenue of history.

To be the only one who was in on the submergee "jokes" that arose while reading the statements of innocent and perplexed biographers, as they attempted to accurately report on their submergee subjects, was sometimes such a hilarious experience that I could barely restrain my inner howls of laughter. This strangely pleasant experience became somewhat dangerous if I happened across an especially delicious example of unusual submergee behavior while reading these biographies in public settings. The joyous and often healing assurances of recognition that came in these private and sometimes public moments of laughter often left me with a wonderful sense of progress and the knowledge that this was time well spent.

After battling bleary eyes and reading through reams of irrelevant material, the real payoff came in those special moments, when the curtains were drawn back in some unexpected manner on a submergee subject, revealing startling behaviors and unique character traits. Sometimes an unusually insightful comment made by the biographer would provide an important clue or fact. Other reference sources such as magazine articles, photos, documentaries and film footage also helped to produce the special kind of evidence I needed to capture. I found the most important tool of the submergee detective was dogged persistence, the willingness to go on and on and on. There were no shortcuts to the finish line, to the completion of the larger body of insights I needed to build based on this study.

One example of the kind of sparkling submergee "gems" that were unearthed through this research work comes from a comparison of two submergee presidents: Ronald Reagan and Harry Truman Following is a list of the behaviors that they had in common:

Both preferred their left hand for some functions, but both used their right hand for writing.

Both had a preference for wearing flashy clothing. Truman's unorthodox ties and "Florida shirts" set him apart from those who preferred everyday attire. Reagan, who had made his living as an actor, liked wearing natty garb and two-tone shoes as much as, if not more than, Truman.

When sight-reading, both read in a monotone, yet both were dynamic speakers when they delivered their material in an extemporaneous fashion.

Both had a strong sense of their personal identity. Of Truman it was said:

Hidden Handedness

In fact, I've never met anyone whose idea of his personal identity was clearer than Truman's. There was nothing passive about this. He seemed to be as interested in ascertaining his exact position in space and time as the pilot of a ship or plane is in ascertaining his.[30]

Both were avid readers with photographic memories.

Both had a fluid and gracious manner of movement that could easily be seen when they walked. Both were very fast walkers. Truman's pace was 120 steps per minute.

Both had a dispensational management style. They enjoyed getting decisions made quickly.

Both made a point of avoiding personal arguments and deferred to others, a practice which helped to build loyalty.

Both of them were noted for their numerous quirks and strange quips that gave the press a real field day.

Sophisticates saw both men as gauche.

Both were populists who "Never met a stranger." Both had a gift for making the common person feel as if he were somehow connected to them.

Neither man was an academic barn burner, but both had the ability to stand off and look at themselves as if they were another person. As President, Reagan played the "role of a lifetime." Truman said he was the President "Whom I happened to be temporarily."

Both were avid swimmers. Reagan was an expert swimmer who swam competitively and had an extraordinary career as a lifeguard. Both men were accomplished horseback riders who loved the sport.

On the surface, both men were characterized by an overall happy or sunny disposition and both formed and maintained strong bonds to their mothers.

Both were very sentimental about the women in their lives, yet they were still masculine characters. Both could be painfully shy in the presence of women with whom they were not already familiar.

Both men had a strong spiritual and moral compass that governed their personal and political lives.

Truman's many submergee behaviors, like Reagan's unique quirks, made the process of researching Harry Truman a pleasant one. Given time, other books covering submergee aspects of figures such as Reagan and Truman really should be written. A rather remarkable example of Truman's submergee handedness in action was demonstrated by his ability to pitch with either hand. On April 18, 1950, at the Washington Senators baseball game, Truman pitched the first pitch of the season twice. One pitch was left-handed and the other was right-handed.

BIOGRAPHICAL BRIDGES TO SUBMERGEES

As my biographical research progressed, I accumulated a small library of submergee history that has served as an invaluable reference source. With this collection at hand, I had a tangible body of data to study. The facts and observations recorded by professional biographers studying characters who were in fact submergees could be used to construct a set of patterns, a series of "bridges" that could link these lives together to form a preliminary outline of submergees in action. The synthesis of facts and patterns formed by these biographical reference points provided me with the important insights I needed to better understand my submergee history and the larger tale of submergees set in the world at large.

I do need to make it clear that direct evidence demonstrating the fact that an individual is a submergee is very rare. Good evidence of submergee status exists in the cases of Presidents Truman and Reagan. But keep in mind the fact that my search for that information was successful only because of the extensive body of information that is available for study on both individuals. The combination of a large body of resource materials, and the lucky fact that the specific data needed to ascertain their submergee history had been recorded, had to occur before the submergee label could be applied with confidence.

The process of deducing whether a famous individual may or may not be a submergee is not a science, it is really an art form in its earliest conceptual state. When I write that someone is a submergee I am normally presenting my opinion. In some very special cases such as with Presidents Truman and Reagan, enough facts are available to report that the individual is in fact a submergee. Given that even the "simple" topic of handedness is itself still shrouded in mystery and controversy, I'm content to present my opinions regarding submergees for what they are; in most cases, a series of somewhat educated guesses.

A wonderful example of the limitations we are faced with when debating adult handedness issues comes from comments made by Professor Chris McManus in his encyclopedic work *Right Hand Left Hand: The Origins of Asymmetry In Brains, Bodies, Atoms And Cultures*.[31] In his book, McManus bemoans the poor academic standards of author James T. de Kay and others who have published claims regarding the left-handed status of famous personalities. McManus then goes on to make statements that contradict those who have published the offending claims (de Kay claims in print that Bob Dylan and Picasso are left-handed) with evidence of his own that "demonstrates" these claims are irresponsible. McManus concludes that "Two such mistakes begin to look like carelessness or worse."[32]

In researching Dylan and Picasso myself to check McManus, I found that the waters regarding the handedness of these two famous figures were muddy, not clear. De Kay, McMannus and the rest of us are caught in a quandary because of the fact that we lack the resources we need in order to discuss these questions with certainty. McManus deserves credit for the investment of time and energy that it took to produce his detailed book, which is a resource text written for academic consumption. Unfortunately, even Professor McManus struggles with limited access to the kind of primary sources, research and data that would make accurate reporting possible on questions such as the handedness of Bob Dylan and Pablo Picasso. The quarry is elusive, meaningful data is rare or nonexistent, and to pretend otherwise is to mislead.

For the moment, in discussing the topic of handedness, writers must point to "famous lefties" as de Kay and others do using data that may or may not be accurate or they may decry the practice as McManus does. Until better understandings and terms are in place and until more precise and reasonably priced non-invasive diagnostic tests for handedness are commonly available, we are reduced to working awkwardly with the very limited resources that are at hand. The waters of handedness are muddy now but they are beginning to clear and, as they do, we will enjoy the opportunity to understand the issue based on facts, not fiction.

During my biographical period, I often felt like a submergee surfer enjoying an endless summer. I surfed along on one perfect wave of insight after another as the *Ah ha's!* of discovery rolled into my awareness with such power and joy that it made each ride a thrill. I have no doubt that those who choose to follow in my footsteps will certainly experience something of the pleasure I felt as I harvested fresh insights on a number of famous submergees. Much of what I had believed about Emperor Napoleon Bonaparte had to be completely revised as I studied his life with new eyes. Similar revisions in my thinking also occurred in connection to Mahatma Gandhi and Mark Twain, both of whom can be understood in a completely different way when seen as submergees.

In the same way that Morris found it was impossible to capture the essence of submergee President Reagan using standard biographical methods, biographers writing about other submergee subjects have been critically handicapped. Lacking the critical insight that they were working with a submergee, they too have had to work in the dark, without being aware that some very unique elements are at work in the body and mind of their subjects.

Hidden Handedness

With the exception of Morris, biographers laboring to accurately portray the inner character and workings of submergees are invariably doomed to serious frustration or dry and factual treatments that miss the mark. In the more specialized biographical treatments by an intimate biographer such as Morris, attempts to delve deeply into the inner world of a subject can become maddening when the object of their study is a submergee. Lacking an understanding of the profound impact that Reagan's submergee status had on his behavior, Morris dug for the essence of President Reagan and found a phantom.

In grappling to faithfully portray the essence of Ronald Reagan, Morris had to find a way to meet the President on his own unique Reaganesque turf. This meeting was something that could only take place if Morris dared to break the rules of his trade, to abandon his role as a traditional biographer and become a fictional character. The fictional Morris worked in this case because he could exist within the strange domain of Reagan's inner life in a manner that Edmund Morris could not. As Morris delved deeper into the submergee nature of President Reagan, creating a fictional self must have seemed less and less absurd, more and more a necessary ingredient of an accurate biography.

Not only in biographies, but in real life, submergee characters perplex those who are in close proximity to them. Observers often report that they find submergees "complex" and "enigmatic." Because they aren't understood, the inner person or essence of a submergee is almost always overlooked, ignored or completely misunderstood. This frustration is particularly evident in the works of talented biographers when they take a submergee as their subject. Morris is a case in point: he was awarded a Pulitzer Prize for his work on President Teddy Roosevelt, yet many readers gave him raspberries for his biography of President Ronald Reagan.

Heroic efforts are called for in order to enter into and attempt to accurately portray the world of a fascinating submergee character like Reagan. Given the submergee subject that Morris tackled in *Dutch*, I should like to be the first to nominate him not for raspberries, but as a candidate for another Pulitzer Prize, this one to be given for this fearless treatment of a submergee president. Even if Morris isn't awarded a Pulitzer, at a minimum, I would like to offer him a word of sincere thanks for his bravery in producing *Dutch*.

A SUBMERGED HISTORY? NOT! ~ CHAPTER 13

I love the man who can smile in trouble, who can gather strength from distress, and grow brave by reaction. 'Tis the business of little minds to shrink, but he whose heart is firm, and whose conscience approves his conduct, will pursue his principles unto death.

Thomas Paine

Cultural bias and ignorance have kept hidden handedness veiled for centuries. Consider the work of Edmund Morris in *Dutch*. With fourteen years of persistent research and unlimited access, it was only by fortunate happenstance that he discovered the letters hidden at the presidential library that provided him with examples of Reagan's early penmanship. With a mountain of information at his disposal and years to review it, a seasoned researcher like Edmund Morris unearthed the key to the strangeness of Reagan, but found it of little use in his attempt to unlock the mystery of the man. Thanks to Morris' relentless search, he could cite Reagan's letters in referring to the President's submergee history, but his ability to draw more insight from that knowledge was constrained by simple ignorance and cultural bias. The same forces that blinded Morris are still in place and they will continue to make submergees invisible until we understand that they exist.

Not only are historians and biographers blinded to submergees, but submergees themselves also tend to give a biased report on their handedness. According to researchers who have studied handedness reversals, the typical answer that a submergee gives when asked about his handedness is *I am ambidextrous* or *I use my left hand for certain things, but not for writing.* Suppose that Morris had asked President Reagan directly, *Are you a reversed lefty?* What would the President have said? The implication given by research is that the respondent would claim that he or she is <u>not</u> left-handed.

147

If I had been asked that same question when I was a deep submergee, I would have responded with full conviction that I was right-handed. To this day, my father still has a hard time claiming his left-handed heritage verbally. He starts by claiming that he uses both hands equally well, but when pressed, admits that he is a lefty. This is a sensitive subject, because it normally is linked to unexamined beliefs and assumptions. In much the same manner that Professor Stanley Coren reports that left-handed individuals prefer to fit in rather than stand out, submergees appear to be motivated by similar preferences.

Based upon the feedback I have received in my interviews of submergees, the correct answer to the question of whether or not the person being interviewed is a submergee isn't likely to surface without detailed questioning. Self reporting is simply not a reliable means of understanding the answer to the question, *Are you or aren't you a submergee?* This situation is exacerbated by deep submergees like me, who have no memories of the period when their handedness reversal took place. When asked, deep submergees will typically insist that they are what they were trained to become, in my case, a right-hander! This barrier to obtaining accurate information from interviews or surveys based on self-reporting means that researchers and historians must understand that even if the reports given by their submergee subjects are offered in good faith, the data they receive may be false.

Interviews of the teachers, parents or others who have participated directly in the switching process that produces submergee children provides yet another window into the world of submergees. Unfortunately, providing accurate evidence might be embarrassing to the one who can offer it, so it's easy to understand that obtaining accurate submergee histories from these sources can be difficult if not impossible. Many teachers and counselors have expressed frustration with the fact that adults responsible for submergee trauma often treat the issue as if it is not an important problem for the child who has been impacted by this abuse.

Submergees can encounter resistance to their attempts to collect accurate evidence regarding their own history of handedness from adults who were involved in the switching process. Our tendency to repress or ignore unpleasant or difficult topics, if possible, is a fact of human nature that can be very distressing. In my case, I was very fortunate to have the support of my parents as I worked to understand the facts of my submergee history. For those submergees who are forced to guess at their past in the absence of direct evidence, a reliable, risk-free and economical diagnostic procedure would represent an invaluable and much needed resource.

A diagnostic tool that is available now that has produced images showing submergee function in the brain is the Positron Emission Tomography scanning device (referred to as PET). This instrument is capable of accurately revealing sites of brain activity. PET scans produce pictures of brain activity as it directs tasks such as speech and handwriting. Unfortunately, PET scans require exposure to radioactive isotopes as well as the use of expensive equipment and highly trained operators. The high costs of PET scans and the risk factors associated with their use limit their value as a routine diagnostic tool.

I will expand on the topic of research and submergees in the next chapter, but in the meantime, let's return to the limits of what biographers can say about submergees in history and consider the work of an exceptional biographer.

ENTER THE EXCEPTIONAL BIOGRAPHER

One of the best examples of a *biographer who got her man* is author and journalist Georgie Anne Geyer. Geyer writes with telling effect about Fidel Castro in *Guerrilla Prince: The Real Story of the Rise and Fall of Fidel*.[33] Geyer's research and the insights that followed were so good that I found myself howling with laughter, as she lifted the masks off "El Jefe" one by one.

The evidence that Fidel is a submergee is strong. Numerous sources refer to Fidel as a left-handed person; however, his education in the Catholic schools of his day meant that as a left-handed child he would have automatically been trained to conform to the nun's right-handed norms. Ample physiological clues of submergee behavior exist including his wild right-handed pitching which was humorously said to require not one, but two catchers. Fidel has shown a lifelong aversion to dancing, which is atypical in this culture, according to Geyer. Numerous photos exist showing Fidel writing with his right hand, but preferring the use of his left hand for other purposes. Equally important, a long list of unique personal quirks and traits which are characteristic of submergees in positions of leadership have enabled Fidel to remain in power as the enigmatic yet charismatic dictator of Cuba.

In order to hunt down her quarry, Geyer notes that she traveled to twenty-eight countries and performed some five hundred interviews seeking to uncover as many facts as possible about Fidel. I would say that, like Morris, Geyer became obsessed with the challenge of truly understanding the inner workings of her subject. Fortunately, Geyer also persisted in her work and refused to give up the hunt.

In her introduction to *Guerrilla Prince* dated June 27, 1990 Geyer writes. . . *That is why I wrote this book: I want everything to be known. I want people to say, after they have read it, "But, of course . . ." And then - "Oh, my God!"*[34]

I was so taken by the high caliber of Geyer's work that I sensed she had iced the cake on the topic of submergee biographies. After more than two years of grueling research, reading biographies by hundreds of other authors, finishing *Guerrilla Prince* made me feel as if I were reading the definitive work on the subject of my study. I sensed that I had finished the work I needed to do, and the biographical fever began to break. Writing with humor and passion to unveil the *something* that made Castro so different, Geyer's work is that of a master. Fortunately for me, her target turned out to be a famous submergee.

Geyer speaks of her fascination with Castro as follows: . . . *Still, why was I driven--for that is the only word--to write this unlikely book and to uncover as many facts as humanly possible about a man whose entire being demanded his not being known? . . . I found that most of the accepted 'truths' about him were either wholly or largely untrue. For the real Fidel Castro, a fascinatingly and ostensibly 'public' person, is really a meticulously secretive and secreted person, a tactical and strategic genius wholly without human principle who guilefully knows how to weave useful myths and spin historical tales--and, much of the time, even he himself believes them.*[35]

I highly recommend *Guerrilla Prince* to anyone who wishes to read the work of a biographer who went the distance with her submergee subject. Geyer used her training as a journalist to aggressively pursue a large body of insights which she then ran through her systems of analysis to patiently strip off the many disguises of Fidel Castro.

Looking at the biographies completed by Morris and Geyer, it's easy to see how subjects like Reagan and Castro can exhaust the resources of all but the most tenacious writers. Morris worked non-stop for fourteen years. Geyer began her process of researching Fidel in 1966, completing her book in 1991, a span of twenty-five years. Both authors refused to give up, refused to be frustrated and shaken off by their impossible-to-capture quarry. Unfortunately, when you set out to capture fairies, you need to have your fairy dust, magic net and the secret word that is their true name. Biographers who wish to hunt for the essence of a submergee subject need specific terms, unique research and a body of specialized knowledge to draw upon. None of these special tools existed when Morris and Geyer began their safaris into the wilds of the submergee jungle.

The fact that both authors successfully produced challenging and informative books about their submergee subjects without knowing the magic "S" word represents an outstanding credit to the profession of biography, which both writers earned many times over.

In retrospect, my biographical obsession had a significant purpose, but it was one that I eventually outgrew for reasons I will share in a moment. I had learned how to sift through reams of biographical materials in order to first determine if the subject of my study was or wasn't likely to be a submergee and later, to search material that would provide key insights into their character. I also found out how tired my eyes could get after spending days on end paging through thick volumes, searching for the clues I needed. When my hunt was successful, the rewards were wonderful. But there were also long periods when the hunt did not go well, when I had to deal with disappointment too.

As I persevered and found more submergee personalities captured by biographers, I catalogued the key information I found for later use. Thanks to that effort, numerous insights gleaned from the history of many famous submergees could be shared with others to illustrate the submergee story. I knew that I had the makings of the most entertaining chapter in my book, an expose of submergees at work in the pages of history.

THE FEVER BREAKS

As my biographical illness ran its course, it wasn't uncommon for me to have from five to twenty books in progress on a single submergee suspect at any given time. Once I began my study, I would read and research everything that was available on the subject. I had become a familiar figure to the local librarians. My research technique was based on a process of becoming immersed in the character I needed to understand. I would dive into the subject's world. The research process continued until I had gained a clear sense of the answer to my primary question: is this famous figure a submergee or can I remove him or her from my list of suspects? Had I been slightly more obsessed with this game of discovery or slightly less impelled to publish my own story, I could easily have spent another five to ten entertaining years or even a lifetime in this manner.

As noted earlier, biographical research focused on finding submergee characteristics consumes large blocks of time, because historians and biographers have not yet begun to look for, index, or catalogue the clues one needs to identify submergees. The key information usually comes tucked into the narrative of biographical materials in the form of quirks or perplexing behaviors that are reported but not understood by the biographer or his sources. Finding the right information in the form of quotes, pertinent narrative or pictures is really a matter of effort and pure chance. As the list of "finds" generated from this research effort grew, my notes outlining the salient characteristics of submergees became better rounded and more detailed. The details I needed to fill in the larger picture I was assembling from the lives of many submergees gradually took shape.

I had been bitten by the submergee biography bug--the same bug that consumed Morris for fourteen years and Geyer for twenty-five. I was sorely tempted to continue my hunt for famous submergees indefinitely, as a much-loved hobby. But my studies had served their purpose and were keeping me from my primary task: bringing the subject of submergees and emergees out into the open, where others could benefit from that knowledge. I was torn between the pleasure of my quest for more submergee insights and the pressing need to tell my story.

I could see that a book, or at the least an extended chapter, regarding the unique aspects of the famous submergees I had studied would be a fun project. However, I knew that emphasis would most certainly distract from my primary objective, which is to tell you the details of the submergee and emergee story as accurately as possible. Beginning to tell the submergee story by trading on its entertainment value and controversy would have been fun, but I concluded that it would be counterproductive and risky to dwell on the history of famous submergees at the expense of telling the everyday and far more important story of submergees and emergees in a responsible manner.

This chapter was originally written as a series of long and unabashedly scandalous tales that detailed the many strange and fascinating acts of famous submergees in history. That chapter would no doubt have titillated and delighted many readers thanks to its ample menu of submergee rogues. Alas, that chapter would also have become a distraction from the main intent of this work, which is a balanced introduction to the subject of submergees. Thankfully, I escaped from the temptation to entertain and titillate, and have instead remained focused on the primary task at hand. With apologies to all who were hoping for something more sensational, I will end with a question and an answer.

A submerged history? Not!

CONNECTING THE DOTS--THE SUBMERGEE PICTURE ~ CHAPTER 14

The results showed just how invisible left-handers are. Based upon the parent's questionnaires, we determined that 9 percent of the mothers and fathers were left-handed in this particular group. Based upon the reports of their high school aged sons and daughters, however, only 4 percent were left-handed. In other words, 56 percent of the left-handed parents went unnoticed by their young-adult children who had lived with their parents for an average of 17 years! In every single case in which a parent's handedness was reported wrongly by the child, a left-handed parent was reported to be right-handed. In not one instance was a right-handed parent reported to be left-handed.[36]

Professor Stanley Coren

The really fascinating part about connecting a series of dots in order to produce a picture, is the way that a detailed picture emerges from what at first appears to be nonsense, a series of unrelated points. In like manner, attempts at producing an accurate picture of submergees is doomed to fail, unless the artist first recognizes the special nature of the subject. If the dots used to draw the submergee picture are placed in the right location and order before they are connected, what would be chaos instead becomes recognizable and familiar.

A UNIQUE MIND-SET

If one were to pick the first dot to start with in creating a picture of submergees, it would have to be the special perceptual viewpoint that they hold. The unique mind-set of submergees can in some cases be a powerful asset for politicians like Presidents Reagan and Truman or Cuban dictator Fidel Castro. Ronald Reagan and Fidel Castro have been marked by their ability to maintain a strong public image, which is made possible by their capacity to forge a strong bond of loyalty in the hearts of those they lead. As the great Communicator, President Reagan had an extraordinary ability to connect to television audiences. Reagan possessed a certain *magic* that enabled him to connect in an almost visceral manner with those who were watching him from the other side of the camera lens. Castro's ability to hold large audiences under his spell and to manipulate public perception and global opinion is still legendary. The arena of politics makes a wonderful stage for submergee leaders.

Examples of this unique character trait in action can be seen in the story of the Cuban missile crisis. Years after the conflict had ended and those on opposite sides of the conflict between the US and the USSR, could compare notes, historians were taken aback by the deft manner in which Fidel Castro had managed to manipulate perceptions on both sides of the conflict. They discovered that Castro had succeeded in stage- managing the two super powers for his own purposes, an amazing feat for the dictator of a small third world power!

Another example of deft political maneuvering exists in the record of President Ronald Reagan, who adroitly managed the levers of statesmanship and public opinion in order to put an end to the cold war.

Looking at these two stories from the outside, one sees a unique capacity for geopolitical maneuvering demonstrated by both men. These two submergee leaders have altered the course of history in a significant manner with their amazing ability to play the game of geopolitics.

Working under the spotlight of public exposure, submergees can be seen utilizing their charisma and charm, something for which they seem to have a special gift. Submergee leaders have a unique capacity to project themselves to the masses that they govern, a skill that enables them to connect on a completely different wavelength. Reagan and Castro both used this skill to frustrate opponents, and engender a sense of loyalty, inclusion, and a shared consensus in those they influenced. With this capacity for inclusion they were able to cast a compelling vision of their programs, which were endorsed by strong majorities.

The potency of submergees in politics is two-fold, because they have a capacity to fuse the near prophetic clarity of their vision of present and future events with an almost messianic and charismatic power to influence others. Both Castro and Reagan demonstrated an almost supernatural capacity to make their causes live in the minds and hearts of those who supported them, while also convincing them that they could be trusted to implement their plan.

Although we don't understand the altered neurology that creates the special political talents of submergee leaders, the unique mind-set of submergees can be a valuable asset in politics. Submergees can use their special ability to see themselves from a distance, to lead in a powerful and charismatic manner, and to forge the sense of an intimate link between themselves and those who follow them. The ability to engender faith, belief and trust in the submergee leader who leads his followers in this way is based on the assurance that their leader knows what is right, and is acting in full accord with their own true inner wishes.

THE INVISIBLE DOT

On a personal level, all submergees have in some sense been exiled from important parts of themselves, from the pieces of self they had to leave behind in order to meet the requirements of living as submergees. Having left behind and forgotten important pieces of their body and mind and past experiences in order to shift their handedness, submergees must cope with an alienation from parts of themselves. This alienation affects the way that submergees inhabit their body and mind. Instead of being at home in their body and mind, they must live in it as an exile or foreigner. The same alienation applies to the submergee thought process, which also has to accommodate the unique demands that are placed on submergees because of the altered patterns of their shifted and less efficient neurological system.

Without a means of understanding their history of handedness, submergees have no way of forming a clear picture of themselves. It's not uncommon to hear a submergee make the claim that they are *just a switched left-hander* or that they are *really ambidextrous*. This statement is typically made in the context of a poor or nonexistent understanding of the power of the submergee experience to alter the submergee's perceptions, or on a larger scale, to comprehend the impact of cultural pressures. In concert with the wonderfully plastic and adaptive nature of their body and mind, submergee children succeed in transitioning to the submergee operating state at a young age, but in doing so, they must *forget* what was left behind. This forgetting process leaves submergees thinking that all is well, that their submergee status is perfectly normal and appropriate, just as I had done before emerging.

It makes sense that as a deep submergee, I would have difficulty understanding that important parts of my self that were abandoned long ago, might still exist. In my case, as a submergee, the proposition would have been that I was really a different person, a left-hander and not the right-hander I thought I was. Without the vantage point of one's own emergee viewpoint to see from, it is impossible to clearly see one's submergee status for what it is. At a minimum, the testimony of a group of emergees is needed, former submergees who can attest that they were in fact exiled in some fashion from their true selves. Without access to that testimony, submergees will have a difficult time seeing a clear picture of their plight, no means of understanding the full magnitude of what has been lost. If the submergee trauma is not perceived, it will be impossible to heal its invisible wounds.

WE ARE INVISIBLE, BUT WE ARE NOT ALONE

Much like submergees, the minority left-handed and ambidextrous populations are largely invisible to the right-handed majority. As Professor Coren has pointed out in *The Left-Hander Syndrome*, the desire of the left-handed and ambidextrous population to fit in as smoothly as possible to a predominantly right-handed society provides a significant reason for this lack of visibility. The desire to fit in is reinforced by the natural tendency of the right-handed majority to presume that other handedness groups should be the same as they are. These two reinforcing desires fuel our tendency not to see left-handers as a genuine minority group. Like any blindness that has persisted for millennia, the problem of invisibility regarding distinctions in handedness has deep roots. The robust stability of our skewed viewpoint on handedness results from the fact that the super majority population status of the First Hand has remained relatively constant throughout human history.

There are at least two social forces that help to reinforce the right-handed status quo: First, the desire to *pass* as if one is no different than the right-handed majority. Second, culture's tendency to encourage or in some cases force the minority to fit into the norms of the majority. These influences are supported by the physical environment because we exist in a world filled with tools and spaces which are predominately designed and built to accommodate the needs of the right-handed majority. In a man-made world that is culturally and physically biased to favor the majority of the First Hand, it's easier to think and act as a right-handed being.

In cultures where differences in handedness are not actively suppressed, members of the Second (left) and Third (ambidextrous) Hand have benefited from a gradual process of recognition and support for their differences and unique needs. Second and Third-Handers are accepted and encouraged to express the uniqueness of their handedness in these cultures. Equally important, the tools and built environments that provide a context for broad-based acceptance of differences in handedness produce a spatial setting that removes many of the physical handcuffs and hurdles that are imposed elsewhere. In those social settings where the second and third-handed are respected as peers with equal rights, enlightened design of manufactured objects and social spaces has followed. As an American emergee who has benefited from some support for this trend in the US, I draw satisfaction from every encounter I have with a design that thoughtfully acknowledges the important role that Second and Third-handed individuals play in our world.

Because submergees are not recognized as a handedness group, they have no unique identity and social standing related to their handedness. They are vulnerable to the powerful shaping currents that originate primarily from the majority status and influence of the First Hand. Submergees who are not grounded in their own unique identity must borrow their sense of what their handedness is from the other groups. The primary insult to self that comes from the experience of being exiled from parts of their body and mind, is aggravated further by cultural pressures to conform to the norms of other handedness groups. Submergees currently exist in the shadow of the three traditional handedness groups, they live without an identity of handedness that flows out of who and what they are.

Stanley Coren illustrates his point about left-handedness and invisibility as follows:

It may be hard to imagine that a set of muscular responses [speaking of left-handed individuals] *that affects virtually every manipulation of the environment, as well as numerous other body movements, could go unnoticed. Yet it does.*[37]

Since our maladaptive views toward handedness have thrived primarily because of ignorance, it will take years of educational effort and social change to finally put an end to the problem. We must find a means to educate ourselves and others. To those who say in blissful ignorance, *Just get over it, because that's just the world as it is,* we need to reply that the submergee trauma can and will be stopped and that in time, solutions can and will be found. We need to *get it* and understand that our handedness is an essential and powerful part of us that shapes our body and mind and the environments we live in. Handedness has a direct connection to our essence, the nuts and bolts of who we are. Drawing in the dot of invisibility on our connect-the-dot portrait of submergees brings a surprising perspective to the process. In fact, once the invisibility barrier is broken down, creating a picture of what submergees are becomes much easier.

DEPRESSION ~ THE SUBMERGEE WHIRLPOOL

I knew from personal experience that my submergee past was characterized by chronic depression. A key marker of my emergee experience was the manner in which I found that I was gradually liberated from this sad state. I use the term *submergee whirlpool* because of the horrible effect that years of living in a state of chronic depression had on me. Looking back on that past, I would say that portions of the innate *neural buoyancy* I now benefit from were missing when I was a submergee. Based on my research of famous submergee figures, a common thread that runs through their lives is depression. A leading question I have learned to ask when interviewing submergees is, *Do you struggle with depression?*

Thankfully, the era has passed when those who are depressed would automatically be subjected to the simplistic statements from well meaning but misinformed individuals, such as, *Just cheer up, it's all in your head*! Increased research into the physiological factors that contribute to depression combined with the development of more effective treatments for this illness has made a real difference in what can and is being done for those who suffer from depression.

While it's not appropriate to make a blanket statement that all submergees are chronically depressed, it would be fair to say that the apparent neurological price of the submergee state includes elements of emotional pressure and physiological trauma that predispose submergees to the illness of depression. The weight of submergee deficits seems to somehow rob the submergee's system of life forces that might otherwise create the kind of upward lift that enables one to live successfully in spite of life's many challenges, to overcome the downward drag and the ugly ravages of depression.

In my early twenties, I was diagnosed with depression and treated with prescription drugs, which helped me to recover. My battle with this monster was profound enough that I attempted to take my life on more than one occasion. Thankfully, I didn't succeed, but I am certain that many submergees have not been so fortunate. Chronic and severe depression can be a killer. In personal terms, I once hated waking up, whereas I now enjoy being alive and find life more colorful, easier to handle, and more rewarding than it once was. Challenges that used to pin me down, leaving me helpless and depressed, are now far less likely to overwhelm me. As the evangelist Ray Brooks once put it regarding our handling of life's struggles, I have been blessed to become an "Over comer" instead of an "Under goer."

A key component of depression is the sense of isolation that seems to come built-in to the submergee state of mind. A superb portrait of this sense of isolation is painted by Eileen Simpson in her book *Reversals*. Submergees who cope with the kind of learning and performance deficits that Simpson's biography describes must do so without the knowledge that the cause of their struggles is something over which they have no control. Submergees lose their internal reference points of self and this loss leaves them powerless to assign blame for their struggles to external causes. Without an inner frame of reference to guide them, submergees suffer because they are unable to see themselves accurately. Simpson illustrates this sense of disconnection from her own pre-submergee history as well as the frustration and confusion that came from struggling against unknown contrary forces. Based on my own experiences with submergee induced depression, I would offer the thought that the systems that were designed to guide and keep us stable and productive in the midst of life's struggles are disconnected to one degree or another by submergee trauma.

The state of *induced amnesia* that characterizes submergee children leaves them defenseless against the belief that they are to blame for their inadequacy, stupidity and clumsiness. The reinforcement process of everyday experiences inexorably drives the submergee child into a whirlpool of internal blame, guilt and shame from which they cannot escape. Once submergees begin to blame themselves for their problems, they have an object to affix blame to and the cruel process begins its work. The submergee whirlpool gains increasing power over its victims as time passes, because the self-perpetuating nature of submergee deficits energizes the engine of depression, increasing the power of its downward pull.

162

THE ONE WHO HAUNTS US

Because submergees are unaware of and cannot understand what they have lost, they must assume that the *what, why,* and *how* of their struggles with depression are based on their own internal flaws. This sense of helplessness and worthlessness alienates the submergee from his empowering internal messages and sense of self. A character, referred to in some circles as the "Inner Critic"[38], gains power from the chronic self-blame and guilt which submergees tend to suffer from. The Inner Critic represents an adversary who can be far more harmful to the submergee's inner self than any external enemy.

The Inner Critic in submergees is energized by an inner *knowing that I can do far more than I am accomplishing*. Without their psychological and physiological wounds, submergees would be capable of a much higher level of performance than the one they exhibit in their less efficient altered state. As a submergee, I lived with a haunting sense of shame, of constantly falling short of goals *I knew I was capable of*. The giant who lived within me was locked up, unable to express himself, but I knew that he existed inside me. The reason for this knowing that I was second best is easy to understand now that I am free to use the talents that were once buried. I had to live with the haunting knowledge that the resources and gifts of a much larger and more capable person existed within me. As a submergee, I was powerless to unearth what had been buried, to put the giant within to work in behalf of my cause of life, until I chose to emerge.

Once this backdrop of forgetting and inner poverty is understood, it should come as no surprise that one of the most common markers that I have learned to associate with the submergee state is chronic depression. In spite of outward appearances, including surprisingly *sunny* dispositions, the tendency to suffer from depression marks submergees. Various manifestations of depression appear to be one of the more reliable dots we can rely upon in drawing an accurate picture of submergees.

Samuel M. Randolph

HOW BIG IS IT, REALLY?

One of the most common questions I am asked is *How many submergees do you suppose are living in the world today?* My original guess was that perhaps one half of one percent or less of the world's population might be submergees. Because of the invisibility factor that has effectively precluded research and discussion, most people would have the impression that submergees are very rare.

My earliest journeys into the dead zone of submergee research reminded me of the story of a certain blind man who was led next to a full-scale sculpture of a blue whale and asked to identify the large object. The blind man makes many attempts at an answer, but he is persistent, and eventually, he manages to work his way around the object, sensing the size and finally the overall form of the creature that is portrayed. As he touches the small eyes and large mouth, then tail and finally the flukes of the statue, a huge form takes shape in his mind and the body of a whale can be conceived. *Aha!* He finally exclaims *Wow! It's really a blue whale!* Like the blind man, I too was forced to operate without seeing the big picture. There was no one who had gone before who could save me from fumbling around in the dark. I didn't have a sighted person who could say, *The world is full of submergees and, boy, are you in for a big surprise!* I had to find my answer to my questions about submergees and population levels in small bits and pieces.

In one of the more telling examples of my experiences with submergees, I recall an unexpected series of encounters that happened in the course of one day. As I was returning my rental car, I mentioned my concern that the person who was waiting on me had a cast on his right arm. The discussion quickly moved to handedness issues and he related the fact that he was actually a submergee. We were overheard by his colleague and she made the same claim, noting that her father had forced her to become right-handed too. Both were submergees!

Leaving the rental car office, I drove to the college pool where I swim laps to drop off some paperwork. As I spoke casually with two of the staff members about my writing project, both of them reported having had handedness reversal experiences as young girls. Again, both were submergees! I left the pool in a bit of a daze and stopped off to pick up a sandwich at the local sub shop. While standing in line, I noticed that the manager who was helping me was left-handed. We visited as he finished making my sub sandwich and he reported his experience as a left-handed member of the Navajo tribe. He had been subjected to repeated submergee training sessions by adult members of his tribe who viewed his left-handedness as a major problem. The submergee training attempts were unsuccessful, but his struggles had been significant enough that strong memories of the conflicts remained. It struck me as an odd fact at the time, that five volunteer reports were offered by four submergees and one person who suffered from submergee training efforts in a time frame of less then two hours.

Regarding the production of young submergees, a number of variables have a bearing on whether or not a child will succumb to submergee training pressures. Some of the variables are the child's sex, genetic heritage, the age at which training pressures are applied and the strength of the training pressures, as well as the child's personality. These variables have to be combined with one's family of origin, as well as the cultural setting that includes schools attended, relatives, and the immediate social group of the child. In those countries where acceptance of left-handed individuals has grown in recent years, the incentive to create young submergees is reduced, resulting in a lower percentage of submergees in the younger age brackets and a higher percentage in the older age ranges.

All of the variables listed above must be correlated with the strength of an individual's handedness. Strength of handedness may have a critical influence on the degree of resistance that will be present when submergee pressures are applied. In interviewing left-handers, it is not at all uncommon to meet someone like the Navajo male I met, whose handedness could not be shifted in spite of repeated submergee training attempts. According to Coren, some 57 percent of the attempts to shift handwriting are successful.

In eight out of ten cases, the training took place before the second or third grade (no later than eight or nine years of age).[39]

The resistance factor to submergee training may simply be a product of personality or will, but it appears more likely to involve the combined influences of sex, personality, strength of handedness and persistence of those who are doing the training as well as the age at which training is started. A certain percentage of any population will continue to function in their innate handedness even if submergee training pressures are extreme, because some individuals have a higher resistance to the effects of these training efforts.

Those studying the issue of handedness expression in various cultures and epochs have found that the percentage of left-handed individuals who are born into any given culture at any given time remains relatively constant. This proves true whether one looks cross-culturally or across time frames of five, fifty, five hundred, or even five thousand years. As highlighted by Chris McManus, there even appears to be a mysterious force which establishes a *set point for left-handedness* related to the birth rate of left-handed individuals which somehow keeps lefties present and accounted for in spite of attempts by the right-handed majority to eliminate the left-handed population from its ranks.

Herein lies a conundrum, since handedness is a polymorphism, yet the proportion of left-handers appears to have been fairly stable for five thousand years, and possibly ten or even a hundred times longer. Since random drift or a small advantage for either the D or the C gene would have eliminated one of them, **some force must maintain both genes in the gene pool** (emphasis mine).

LEFT HAND RIGHT HAND Professor Chris McManus[40]

If a mysterious force exists in the human race that somehow regulates against extinction of the left-handed population, it would seem that an important purpose might be served by the minority. The presence of this governing force begs a pair of questions for which I have no answers. Why is there an apparent "need" for humans to have a left-handed population present in their ranks? If

166

it's true that the left-handed segment is built in and preserved by some mysterious force, how do the hidden parts of handedness, the Fourth and Fifth Hands fit into this picture?

HANDEDNESS: IS IT REALLY A MATTER OF CULTURE?

A question that every culture is faced with is whether it will embrace its incoming crop of children as they are, or instead attempt to conform them to their culture's accepted norms for handedness. If one were to draw a comprehensive map showing the various countries of the world and rating them on the basis of hospitality or hostility to left-handedness, the difference between countries would be shocking. An example given by Stanley Coren of a country that is harsh on its left-handed population is Taiwan, which he contrasts to the more favorable cultural settings of the US and Canada. This is a loaded topic, but suffice it to say that if an international rating system indexed to cultural acceptance of the various forms of handedness were consulted, that index would show that a proportionately small number of countries exist where Second and Third Handed children are encouraged and supported. The same index would show that a much larger number of countries are not warm and cozy places to live if one is not right-handed. One of the countries where real progress has been made is Germany, once one of the most inhospitable places for the left-handed.

A good example of how bad the situation actually is can be found in the schools of the US. This report came from my niece, who reported an incident that took place in the fall of 2000 while she was completing classes in her senior year of undergraduate work in the school's teacher training program. One of her classmates, who was also finishing her senior year in the program casually told her that she was engaged in switching her child's handedness, never thinking about the damage she was doing.

If graduates emerging from the ranks of our teacher training programs in American colleges aren't learning that creation of more submergee children is a really bad idea, how can we claim that the problem has been addressed adequately in the US? America is thought to be a moderately safe place on the world map of handedness, but on closer examination it becomes apparent that changes made relative to the sanctity of children's handedness have largely been ideological or piecemeal in nature. In the absence of training and curriculum that act directly to address and remedy the submergee problem, the US lags behind more enlightened countries like Germany, where concrete steps have been taken to make the educational system more hospitable to the left-handed.

Professor Stanley Coren reported on data developed from two studies in which he participated. The studies isolated 52 individuals in one case and 31 individuals in the second. The report gives the following results:

The first thing we found was that attempts to change the handedness of left-handers were quite common. . . . Overall, left-handers were successfully shifted in only about two out of every five cases (41 percent). The greatest success came for handwriting, which was successfully shifted in 57 percent of the cases. Of the people who did successfully shift their handedness from left to right, it seems that the trick was to start the training process quite early.[41]

According to Coren, the Chinese culture is one in which the submergee training pressures are particularly strong. The combination of persistence in the training process and an early age of onset were responsible for the conversion of approximately four out of five left-handed Taiwanese children.[42]

Coren's information is particularly welcome because it represents a direct and focused collection of data that compares the submergee populations in various national settings. The statistics cited provide a comparison between the *higher* success rate for switching of handedness that occurred in Chinese culture to the relatively *lower* success rate for switching handedness from left to right amongst children living in the US.

RESEARCH AND HANDEDNESS

Research work completed by Marian Annette and her associates at the Department of Psychology, Leicester University, and more recent findings by James Steele (Department of Archeology, University of Southampton) and Simon Mays (Ancient Monuments Lab, English Heritage) allow us to look at the question of handedness percentages in human population from another vantage point. First, the findings of Annette are cited by Steele & Mays:

A systematic study of the distribution of manipulative skill has been carried out by Marian Annette and colleagues from the Department of Psychology at Leicester University. Annette and Kilshaw (1983) in a group of 1480 adolescents and adults, using a simple peg-moving task apparatus to assay hand skill, 82% or more were skilled with the right hand, 3% were equally skilled with each hand, and 15% were more skilled with a left hand. When that disparity of skill between the two hands is plotted as a histogram, it becomes apparent that skill asymmetry is normally distributed: there is no clear separation in the two conventional handedness groups.[43]

Annette's group found a continuum of performance differences in their peg moving tests. Annette's work supports a bell curve model of handedness strengths in which some 15% of the population exits on the left side of the curve, with 3% in the center and 82% on the right (Note, while a classic bell curve was used to model handedness population, the central axis of ambidexterity is shifted to the left in order to accommodate the larger proportion of right-handed individuals). Returning to the report findings of Steele and Mays:

Steele and Mays took measurements of the lengths of the humerus and the radius in adult medieval skeletons excavated from the cemetery of the medieval village of Wharram Percy, in Yorkshire. They reasoned that this would give the best skeletal indicator of arm length . . . Of the 80 adults whose bones are sufficiently complete to be measured, 81% were longer in the right arm, 3% were of equal length on each side, and 16% were longer in the left arm. Furthermore, the histogram of arm length asymmetries had the same shape as that plotted for Annette and Kilshaw's contemporary data . . .

Data from a 1930's study of arm length asymmetry in adult human skeletons from different regional populations of the world (Schultz 1937) give a pooled mean of 79% longer in the right arm, 3% of equal length on either side, and 18% longer on the left side--results strikingly similar to those found by Steele and Mays and by Annette and Kilshaw using the behavioral measure.[44]

When the findings of these studies are compared, the percentages of those who would prefer to be left-handed in the groups studied remained surprisingly constant. The work of Steele and Mays underscores the strong probability that handedness is expressed in similar percentages across cultures and time. The key variable, it appears, is the attitude towards handedness in the culture being studied.

The generally accepted figures that are currently used to quantify the left-handed population in the United States show that an average of 11% of the male population and 9% of the female population fit this category. Combining the two figures results in an average of some 10% of Americans who are left-handers. This 10% figure contrasts with an average of some 15% to 18% of any population that would prefer to be left-handed before cultural pressures are applied based on the combined data developed by Steele & Mays, Annette and other researchers.

Using the most conservative figure from the ranges developed above, this crude extraction gives an aggregate group of roughly 5% of the US population that could be classified as submergees with a fair degree of confidence. Keep in mind the fact that we think of the United States as a moderately safe haven for left-handed people to live, a place where individual freedoms including the right to grow up and express one's innate handedness are supposedly protected.

The submergee problem is consistently reported as *much worse* or even *severe* in other countries where left-handedness is still strongly discouraged. Studies by Asian researchers have shown that anti left-handed bias is particularly strong in China, Taiwan and Japan. However, the submergee phenomenon impacts every country and every culture to one degree or another.

My answer to everyone's favorite question about the current size of the submergee population worldwide is based on the facts as I now understand them. An aggregate of some three to five percent of the US population appears to be submergees. Based on shifting cultural attitudes in some countries, the percentages of submergees appear to be higher in older age groups and lower in the younger age categories. In some parts of the world where left-handedness is viewed with real distaste, these same numbers may rise as high as ten to thirteen percent. On that basis, a range of between three to thirteen percent of any given population worldwide can potentially be classified as submergees.

When the dots that can be extracted from research on handedness populations are all connected to generate an estimate of just how big the world's population of submergees must be, the picture that emerges shows that a significant segment of humans now living on this planet are submergees.

THE BIG TOE

A favorite joke of mine is posed in the form of a question: What three and a half pound object spends almost all of its time trying to figure out what it is? The answer is our brain, the single most curious piece of matter in the universe. My brain experienced a big boost in its curiosity quotient once I became an emergee. I would now describe myself as *incurably curious*. Fueling this wide-eyed state, I have an almost insatiable desire to understand what happened to me when I emerged and what made it possible, a desire that will probably mark me for the rest of my life. The principle object of my curiosity is what I refer to as the Big Theory of Everything (Big TOE) regarding submergees and emergees. I just have to know how the body and mind can accommodate submergee and emergee shifts. I admit that my goal is ambitious, but curiosity drives my search for answers.

One theory that seems to give the right answers to those searching for the Big TOE is that our lateralization preferences are actually encoded at conception. If this is true, genetic coding governs one's laterality to a degree that is far more influential than many had once thought possible. It is as if a dynamic set of blueprints are drawn up for each of us at conception in order to govern the laterality and function of our body and mind. The genetic benchmark that determines an individual's lateralization appears to be pre-determined. Thus, altering or tilting this balance of laterality in submergees detours the organizing process that guides the chain of developmental events that determines laterality and handedness. Submerging an individual fundamentally changes and retargets the developmental process from its original design to a less than optimal alternate outcome.

In contrast to the process of detouring that creates submergees, an emergee is actually collaborating with the guidance systems that were overridden in childhood by handedness conversion. My premise is that the design for left-handedness that existed in my genes at conception made my emergee return possible, even though that return took place decades after conception. My reasoning is guided by the fact that I experienced much higher body and mind function as a direct result of the emergee journey. Some form of a *force* kept my emergee processing systems all swept and clean, waiting in good order for my return. All I did to emerge was turn the key to the door of handedness and this well-preserved *force* did the rest. Granted, I am only working with a sample of one in forming my model of what the emergee process is, but my experience tells me that a dynamic guidance system or blueprint of some sort was activated by my altered behaviors and this served to guide me on my way once I set out on my emergee journey.

Following is a rough outline of the two processes that takes place in the formation of submergees and emergees, as I now understand it.

A Sketch of the Journey Taken By Submergees and Emergees

The submergee formula appears to work in the following manner (for a left-handed individual):

1. Normal development of skills occurs until submergee training takes place.

2. A submergee *Shift* of activity (handwriting, etc.) takes place from the preferred left hand to the non-preferred right hand.

3. A concurrent *Shift* of brain function takes place in which pre-existing patterns in the formerly dominant hemisphere are called upon to inform cortex activity in newly activated areas in the opposite (auxiliary) hemisphere.

4. The pre-existing neural patterns in the formerly dominant hemisphere continue to serve some purpose based upon their prior roles, thus the neurons utilized for this purpose are maintained in working order. The pruning of neurons that would normally take place due to this reallocation of resources does not occur.

    Stop the process here. Most submergees remain in this state for life unless a decision is made to return, to emerge.

5. Time passes and at some point many years later, an emergee *Shift* of activity (handwriting, etc.) takes place in the opposite direction. Dominant function for handwriting and other skilled activities is moved back from the right hand to the left hand.

6. In order to support this change in the weight of use, a concurrent *Shift* of brain function occurs in reverse in which innate body and mind efficiency is regained.

7. Based on my experience, as a consequence of restored processing efficiencies, a rebound effect occurs in the body and mind of the emergee, resulting in enhanced perception and function.

No doubt there will eventually be many other theories offered to explain what really is taking place in submergee and emergee experiences. I look forward to seeing these other explanations as they surface. For the moment however, I believe that the concepts offered above represent a plausible working model for the events being considered here.

Recent findings in genetic research provide us with some of the best hints of what this field will have to offer submergees and emergees in the years ahead.

. . . Genes are not puppet masters or blueprints, nor are they just the carriers of heredity. They are active during life; they switch one another on and off; they respond to the environment . . . They are both the cause and the consequence of our actions.

WHAT MAKES YOU WHO YOU ARE Matt Ridley. Time Magazine June 2, 2003.

We know that the patterns of body and mind encoded at conception persistently serve to guide development, both in utero and in the months and years following birth. However, we must now update our static models of gene function based upon recent and rather provocative findings. The startling discovery that our genetic systems are not static, but are in fact interactive mechanisms, brings a new element to consider in resolving the mystery of what makes submergees and emergees. Could it be that genetics holds the key that will unlock the secrets of the mysterious force governing handedness populations that McMannus writes about? Are genetics also the key influence that enable and govern the submergee and emergee process?

We now know that our genes play a much more complex role than we once thought they did. One example is the fact that in humans, laterality issues are resolved, even before the neurons of the brain are connected to the spinal cord at approximately 10 weeks following conception. Citing work completed by Peter Hepper of the Queen's University of Belfast, Chris McManus writes:

Hepper looked at fetuses of only ten weeks gestation . . . In eighty-five percent of the fetuses, it proved to be the right arm [that was moving] . . . This could not be taken as an indication that the brain becomes asymmetric earlier than previously thought, because so early in development the neurones in the brain have not yet become connected to the spinal cord . . . raising the possibility that handedness is not to do with the cortex of the brain but comes from much lower down in the nervous system, although how and where this might be is still not known at the moment.[45]

Now that we can look all the way back to a time frame that is separated by just ten weeks from the date of conception and find evidence of lateralization that arises from something "lower down in the nervous system," we need to ask a question: *If laterality is expressed at this very early stage, then isn't there a very distinct possibility that the programs that determine our laterality are actually created on the very first rung of the developmental ladder?* This early date implies that laterality results from the union of genetic code that takes place at conception.

If it is true that the body and mind conserve neurons from pruning in the face of submergee pressures, the conservation may be taking place because genetic design forces this outcome. Conservation would explain the body and mind's capacity to manifest the incredible late plasticity that makes an emergee return possible. In the event that submergee and emergee shifts do occur, the body and mind somehow *know* how to conserve their initial reference points, which serve to stabilize the shifted system, enabling submergees to function successfully. The force of conservation appears to make submergee function possible and, later, to enable emergee recovery in adults.

One could think of the submergee and emergee journey as a high wire act and the force of conservation as the balancing bar used by the high wire artist to maintain his or her stability. As skilled functions are transferred from one hand to the other during submergee and emergee transitions, the conserved *reference points* of existing skills and experience provide the submergee with a system that allows his body and mind to accommodate the destabilizing pressures of a transition in handedness, while maintaining functionality. When seen as an illustration of human capacity for plasticity, the ability of submergee children to endure a transformation of this magnitude is impressive. The really marvelous part of this story is that somehow the body and mind of

175

children can endure the trauma of being trained to become a submergee without a catastrophic loss of function.

HEMISPHERIC SHIFTS AND SUBMERGEES

The night is quiet; the streets are still; in this house my dear one used to live. She has left the town long since, but the house still stands in the same place. Another man stands there, and stares aloft, and wrings his hands with the weight of grief. I am filled with horror when I see his face; the moon shows me my own features.

You ghostly double, pale companion! Why do you ape the pain of love that tortured me in this place, full many a night in time gone by?

Der Doppelganger (The Ghostly Double, based on the text of Heinrich Heine) a lieder composed by Franz Schubert in the last year of his life.

In accommodating conversion of his or her handedness, the submergee child must somehow manage to shift hand dominance from one side of the body to the other. This feat of accommodation can only be achieved by recruiting the enabling neurological systems in the opposite hemisphere. The neurological shift that takes place in the developing submergee child is a phenomenon that remains hidden to the adults who are directly influencing the transition, or simply refusing to intervene and stop it. The transfer of neurological control in the child's hemispheres must be supported and coordinated by the connecting tissues of the corpus callosum. Henceforth, the neural signals of the submergee brain that once traveled efficiently between hemispheres on the connecting system of the corpus callosum will be subject to the heavier signal traffic required to support transferred control of the hemispheres. Once this transfer of control takes place, the submergee will suffer from a loss in processing efficiency in the brain, caused by the permanent neural bottleneck, or traffic jam, that has been created between their hemispheres.

The loss in efficiency that results from this submergee bottleneck can be illustrated using a neurological test that compares

Interhemispheric Transfer Times (ITT) between one hemisphere and the other in normal subjects. ITT testing documents the fact that processing efficiencies (speed of transfer) are significantly reduced when a stimulus is presented to the non-dominant hemisphere, versus presentation to the dominant hemisphere. The ITT test demonstrates the fact that when the brain is tasked with processing signals that originate in the non-dominant hemisphere, its processing efficiency is reduced. This loss of efficiency can be measured in slower reaction speeds.[46]

More recent testing has illustrated the same principal of reduced processing efficiency using data from animal studies. In relation to submergees, this research supports the understanding that submergees suffer from reduced processing efficiencies due to lower ITT rates. This compromise in ITT efficiency, which is forced on the submergee's body and mind, represents an artificial tax or toll that places an added burden on the neural and physical resources of the submergee.[47]

Numerous examples exist that demonstrate the mind's ability to preserve or conserve itself when faced with extremely traumatic circumstances. This mechanism of self-preservation is at work in cases of Dissociative Identity Disorder (DID), also referred to as Multiple Personality Disorder (MPD). In cases of this kind, one or more "alter" personas may manifest themselves in a single individual. As documented in the following case, the hemispheric and handedness shifts seen in submergees can and do take place in other contexts:

In a study by Polly Henninger of Cal Tech, reports on shifts in hemispheric dominance are associated with shifts in personas. The paper, titled CONDITIONAL HANDEDNESS: HANDEDNESS CHANGES IN MULTIPLE PERSONALITY DISORDERED SUBJECT REFLECT SHIFT IN HEMISPHERIC DOMINANCE details observations of handedness changes that were observed in concert with the various personas of a patient with MPD. Henninger states that:

The handedness changes shown in multiple personality disordered persons are unexpected and suggest a relationship between MPD and lateralized functioning. If abuse leads to dissociation, it is likely to be a child alter that is left-handed, lateralized to the right hemisphere, and dissociated from the verbal awareness of an adult right-handed host personality that is right-handed and lateralized to the left hemisphere.

The paper then goes on to document the testing that verified that this switching had indeed taken place by measuring comparative performance of lateralized tasks between personas respective to their left and right handed dominance. In her concluding discussion, Henninger goes on to make the following statements:

P.G. was initially a left-handed person forced to acquire right-handed skills [a submergee]. *Given her history of abusive parenting, the forced switching could be a significant part of the abuse . . . Although P.G. has developed motor centers in both hemispheres and is capable of shifting control of processing from one hemisphere to the other, at no time does she manifest her ambidexterity. Her manual preference and manual skill are conditional upon which personality is in control. Pe's* voice change to that of a child when she was required to use her opposite hand suggests that the use of a particular hand may be important for maintaining the integrity of the personality in control. The proprioceptive cues and sensory stimulation may help to reinforce the appropriate personality and to maintain the differentiation between personalities . . .*

. . . The high incidence of conditional handedness patients with MPD indicates that P.G.'s case is not an isolated one and suggests a relationship between brain organization and the development of multiple personalities as a means of coping with trauma. It is proposed that early severe trauma in some cases leads to the development of an extreme form of hemisphericity, marked by conditional handedness as a means of escaping the emotional pain.[48]

* (Pe is Henninger's reference to the alter to P.G.)

In addition to interhemispheric switching in humans seen in MPD cases, an article in the May 1999 edition of Scientific American reported on unihemispheric sleep in ducks. The common link between ducks and certain aquatic mammals, who keep one side moving while resting, is a control mechanism that allows one hemisphere to rest while the other one remains awake. Quoting from the article:

The coexistence of two states of consciousness is impressive enough, "but the kicker," Indiana State researcher Niels Rattenborg says, "is the control. Because the bird's brains process some information independently while awake". . .[49]

Two additional insights from neurological researchers may have a direct bearing on our views of hemispheric shifts in submergees. First, the understanding that the human mind is far more plastic than we had thought it was as recently as fifteen years ago. Second, the sharp detail with which the inner workings of the body and mind can now be seen. The body and mind are now viewed as a far more malleable, massively complex, robust and individualized system then we had once assumed they were.

Regarding plasticity, Oliver Sacks, MD writes about the human body and mind:

Thus body-image is not fixed, as a mechanical, static neurology would suppose; body image is dynamic and plastic--it must be remodeled, updated all the time, and can reorganize itself radically with the contingencies of experience. "Cortical representational maps in adults are 'use dependent'" writes Merzenich; they "operate dynamically throughout life." Body-image is not something fixed a priori in the brain, but a process adapting itself all the time to experience.[50]

Regarding our growing appreciation of the complexity at work in the human brain, as Roger Sperry of Cal Tech put it:

Actually, the more we learn, the more complex becomes the picture for predictions regarding any one individual, and the more it seems to reinforce the conclusion that the kind of unique individuality we each carry around in our inherent brain wiring makes that of fingerprints or facial features appear gross and simple by comparison. The need for educational tests and policy measures to selectively identify, accommodate, and serve the differentially specialized forms of intellectual potential becomes increasingly evident.[51]

With those last two insights in view, the larger picture of what submergees really are is framed by the fact that the complex human mind can accommodate and endure a reversal in its dominant laterality. The thought that a return from the submergee state is even possible is surprising, but this is no less amazing than the fact that submergee conversions of humans are possible in the first place. The idea that the body and mind can accommodate submergee function and emergee recovery becomes believable, once current understandings of the system's marvelous resources and plasticity are taken into account.

It is one of life's more amazing facts that an insult to self as deep as a submergee trauma doesn't completely destroy the children who are twisted and reshaped in this manner. Submergees who grow up and manage to find a way to offer their unique talents and gifts to our world are a testimony to the marvelous and resilient systems of the body and mind. Explanations of these complex and robust systems, mechanisms that can endure submergee pressures for decades yet still guide an emergee safely home evoke the artistry of a super intellect, the hand of a Designer.

. . . after a lifetime of conditioning, I, like most left-handers, can get through the day in a world I never made without once being self-conscious about my impediment, much less demonstrating it. (My wife confesses a chronic unease at what she terms my "awkwardness" in the kitchen . . .)

From all of this I have emerged with nothing more disabling than the mildest identity crisis. When asked, on those rare occasions where it seems somehow to matter, I never know what to say but stand, metaphorically, in the open closet doorway, smiling nervously and rubbing my guilty hands together like Pilate.[52]

The Origins & Consequences Of Being Left-Handed - Jack Fincher

The news spread quickly when Dr. Robert Ballard announced that the wreck of the Titanic had been found on September 1, 1985. Soon, everyone in the world could see images of the Titanic where it had come to rest on the ocean floor. The massive ship disappeared without a trace into the cold dark waters of the North Atlantic on April 15, 1912 at 2:20 AM. At the time of its sinking, the Titanic was the largest moving object in the world and one of the most luxurious, yet it had lain in the darkness, undetected and undisturbed for more than seventy years.

The world's media outlets seized on the high voltage story, announcing *THE TITANIC HAS BEEN FOUND!* The news became an obsession for many, one that grew stronger by the day as television, books and magazines revived the history of the famous ship, embellishing the legend of the "unsinkable ship" that sank on its maiden voyage. The legend of the Titanic grew to epic proportions in the hands of Director James Cameron, when the film *TITANIC* earned eleven Academy awards in 1997.

The image of a massive ship that lay hidden from sight for so long, more than two and half miles below the surface of the Atlantic Ocean serves as a powerful link to the world of submergees. When the Titanic sank, more then 1,500 souls perished. When a submergee sinks into the fourth state of handedness, they must leave behind parts of themselves forever, a disaster that can't be seen, but one that is just as real as the sinking of the Titanic. How shall we react to this much larger disaster story once we understand that millions of submergees live in our midst?

The mere mention of the word Titanic evokes in us thoughts of epic disaster and tragedy at a grand scale. The word submergee should have the same effect too since it connects us to a far larger and more immediate tragedy. Submergees represent millions, not thousands, of people, a massive segment of humanity whose lives have been altered forever by a seemingly innocuous event in their childhood.

The ongoing creation of submergee children who grow up to become struggling adults is a disaster story that is in certain aspects equal to the great plagues. The insidious feature of this problem is that we can't see it, have no words to discuss it, and in large part are totally unaware of it. Looking at just one example of the costs of the submergee state to humanity, if the chronic depression caused by submergee trauma is too much and the pressures of life are too intense, the submergee wound can sometimes lead to suicide, nervous breakdown and debilitating personal handicaps. Depression is just one cost of the submergee problem. Add in the fact that we are social creatures, that we are all interconnected, and the true costs of this loss are incalculable. The submergee wounds that humanity continues to bequeath on its offspring either dampen or snuff out God-given gifts that would otherwise have expressed themselves in enhanced and more vigorous lives. As the scale of this tragedy finally comes into plain view, it is appropriate to ask, *How shall we put an end to this living nightmare, this plague on humanity?*

THE SUBMERGEE FACTORY

If there was a factory that created submergee children, the most obvious solution would be to shut the factory down as quickly as possible. It's tempting to think this way, because it's easy to believe that by closing down the factory, we are solving the problem in the most efficient manner possible. The thought process that supports this line of action is something like this: *Fix the problem at its source and then work outward from there.* The problem with this kind of thinking is that it misses the real question, which is: *How do we take this monster problem on at the level and intensity that we need to in order to put an end to it forever?*

The truth is that submergee factories exist in such huge numbers worldwide that it would take several lifetimes to shut them all down unless the issue captures attention worldwide and at the level of interest that the Titanic story did. Keep in mind the fact that our factories have been producing their submergee products for centuries. The issue is bigger than our schools; it includes adults, culture and history itself.

The traditions that create submergee children have thrived without challenge for centuries, plaguing humanity in the main because of ignorance, not malice. If ignorance is the problem, telling the story of our world's submergee population to as many people as possible is the only approach that will work in our lifetimes. Because of the character, size and persistence of this problem, it can't be solved piecemeal. Instead, the issue has to be attacked from the top down by opening the eyes and hearts of the world. The challenge of getting the story out isn't all that tough, once a clear and consistent message is available. Anyone who can count to five can discuss the issue of five types of handedness and explain the message of handedness reversals to others.

OUR SCHOOLS ARE AN EPICENTER

There is a strong motivation to provide what's best for students amongst those who serve in our educational systems. An outstanding body of professionals, parents and interested lay people are in place who are eager to find more effective ways to overcome the persistent problems that educators are faced with. The changes we could readily make in our schools to resolve the submergee problem forever make the academic category a prime zone for change. All that is lacking is a clear understanding of the problem and the leadership to make sure that the problem is solved. The relatively low cost and ease of achieving near term success makes our schools a natural action point.

As over-burdened as schools already are, eliminating an unnecessary source of problems would give a much-needed boost to a system that could use a helping hand. Children who would otherwise have been a drag on school resources will instead be free to participate as productive and vigorous members of the school's student body. The fact that our school systems could benefit from a simple change of policy that would reduce the burden of problem children, while at the same time producing more capable students, is exciting.

The target group for immediate change would be children aged from four to approximately eight years of age (grades K to 3 in the US). Identical changes are urgently needed in schools and homes around the globe irrespective of race, sex or cultural climate. A single clear and consistent change of elementary school policy and a curriculum that respects the innate handedness of students is needed. The new policies should trigger intervention as required in order to stop submergee training and, if needed, provide for remedial therapy. If this single target for change were realized, it would put a serious dent in the submergee problem by focusing on the zone where the epidemic must flourish in order to exist.

One of the primary questions voiced by educators who are familiar with my concerns is *Where do I go for help?* Hopefully, the most critical need, which is to raise awareness and initiate discussion will be addressed successfully by this book. Individuals who become aware of the need for change and who then go on to inform themselves and others will initiate the most important change needed. Next, the social and professional networks that need to be built must to be constructed. I hope to assist in that purpose by offering updates, articles and links to relevant resources (see www.hiddenhandedness.com). Another source in the US that offers resources in English is the Handedness Research Institute (see www.handedness.org).

Growing interest in resolving submergee issues in schools and culture can be observed on the international scene. For those with German language skills, the work of Johanna Barbara Sattler, PhD will be of significant interest. Some of the work done by Sattler has been translated into English. Sattler's clinical experiences with submergees, supplemented by a fairly strong library of resources, should make her organization an important resource that will help to speed the pace of progress. Sattler's organization can be accessed (see www.lefthander-consulting.org).

As illustrated by my own frustrated attempts to find help in the form of well-developed reference and resource information sources, the critically needed connections to help are currently just out of reach, over the horizon. This is a pregnant moment because a whole new world awaits those who wish to explore issues connected to submergees and emergees.

GET OUT OF JAIL - FREE!

Submergee adults who have been trained to become false right-handers are a much larger and more difficult group to reach than young children with the same history. Even though they've been imprisoned for many years, it's reasonable to assume that many submergee adults will choose to remain as-is, in a familiar state where they feel comfortable. Using my own case as an example, I considered myself a right-handed person for forty years and I was settled firmly in that identity. In order for me to emerge from the force of that well-established identity and those habits, I needed help. The forces that wanted to undo what had been done forty years before and the "rebound effect" that took over as that release got underway gave me the critical boost I needed to get the job done.

Is it possible for others, particularly adult submergees to have the beneficial emergee experiences I have described? What appears to take place, as one emerges from submergee status, resembles an accelerated morphing of self in the emergee, a rather novel concept to be advancing. Fortunately, thanks to the exposure of modern societies to the special effects technology of modern media, our culture is better prepared than ever to understand and embrace processes that are based upon accelerated change. The capacity to manipulate images using digital technologies has opened the door of our imaginations to characters that can quickly switch, swap, morph and otherwise change their physical identities and capabilities with ease. The difference is, the emergee experience happens in the real world, not on a theater screen. In this context, the idea that a different and more powerful self resides within the submergee body and mind, ready to appear if asked, is a fairly tame one.

I had spent forty years becoming the submergee that I was and I suppose you could argue that forty more years will be needed in order to fully unravel that history. Unfortunately, we can't travel backwards in time to make that happen. The powerful and complex process of transformation at work in our body and mind that makes us who we are is irreversible. I had a choice: to remain unchanged, a submergee, or to become something new, an emergee. The solution I finally chose in becoming an emergee lay not in an *undoing* of the old self, to become left-handed as I had expected, but in something more, in an accelerated process of transformation that birthed a more integrated person, an emergee.

CONSIDERING THE RISKS

Submergees who choose to emerge will have to leave behind the familiar parts of self that connect them to their submergee identity. The established habits that we form as we settle in and become stable adults represent a fixed set of assumptions that will be impacted in varying degrees by an emergee experience. Additional considerations that adult submergees need to consider relative to the emergee journey include questions of risk. If powerful forces of change will be encountered in an emergee shift, and if little is known about those forces, isn't there a real risk associated with venturing into the unknown?

It may be that far fewer submergee adults will choose the emergee pathway than I might suppose because of the threat to self that it represents. However, if a submergee only goes so far as to seriously consider the possibility of emerging and then decides not to, I believe that much understanding can be gained through this process of self-analysis. Forming a new understanding of one's true past can itself be a gift of great value. Those submergees who seriously engage in the process of evaluating the details of their unique past, yet choose to remain in the submergee state will at a minimum emerge with fresh wisdom and insight. By facing the past that has shaped them into submergees and appreciating their unique gifts and status "as is" they, too, can have an experience that will make their lives much richer.

One fact I have learned to keep in mind based on many one-on-one encounters with submergees is that the idea of making an emergee jump is usually very frightening to those who are qualified to consider making it. Keep in mind the fact that submergees have already had to struggle at a young age in order to compensate for a disorienting shift in their body and mind. In discussing the possibility of emerging, working with submergees, I often get the sense that I am leading them to a cliff and inviting them to jump off into the water far below. As they look down and consider the idea of cliff diving, the fact that I am dripping wet and smiling doesn't seem to help a bit.

Because the submergee training process normally happens at an early age, the memories that might otherwise stimulate a decision to become an emergee are repressed or hidden altogether. I might have balked at the idea of becoming an emergee if it were presented to me by others. Had I not had the benefit of my own eye-opening *Aha!* experience as a submergee which convinced me that I was actually left-handed and thus obligated to act, my story might have had a different ending. In the absence of the kind of insights and confirmation from parents that I benefited from, I have to wonder what my reaction would have been to the claims of a book like this one.

While I was initially very surprised that other submergees didn't quickly see the logic of my emergee choice and follow suit, their reservations exposed the need for a more comprehensive presentation of the case for emerging. Adult submergees need to have a means of gaining enough perspective to make an informed decision, whether to stay put or make the jump to emergee status. A book was needed that would speak to submergees looking for a place to start their own research. The book would have to encompass enough of the subject to give its readers a sense of comfort with the issue, and in addition, I knew that I needed to share a few of the details of my emergee experiences. In the next chapter, I'll also share my thinking on the pro's and con's of emerging.

If one is to abandon one's familiar laterality for some kind of new-fangled version of body and mind, the sensible consumer will shop around first and consider the alternatives. One of the most appealing alternatives, of course, is the comfort of the status quo. I understand very clearly that I can only be responsible for my own choices and with that in mind, I recognize the pioneering nature of what I chose to do and the risks that are associated with exploring uncharted territory. In choosing to emerge, I could have easily gotten into trouble. For that reason, I have chosen to do what pioneers do, develop trail markers to serve those who choose to follow me of their own free will, who choose to accept full responsibility for their decision to strike out and explore the territory of emergees. Frankly, I'm not in a position to say whether or not emerging is a good idea for anyone else, but I can share my story knowing that I am contributing something that will help to fill in the void that I encountered when I made my decision to emerge.

Remaining in the familiar state of the submergee body and mind represents a sane and in some ways safer and more appealing state of affairs than the alternative does. I am guessing that any submergee who determines that he or she has sufficient incentive to make the emergee jump will do so by establishing a direct link between their submergee trauma and specific personal struggles. Someone like this may also find that they simply *know* that an emergee return is right for them, as I did. In order for an accurate linkage of trauma to disability to occur, it's critically important for adult submergees to develop an accurate assessment of their past. Diagnostic tools and trained counselors are urgently needed to make this less of an art and more of a science than it is presently. It goes without saying that specialized therapeutic resources geared to meet the specific needs of submergees are needed, but to my knowledge, as of this moment they are unavailable. My advice as of this moment to submergees? *Caveat Emptor!* (literally, "buyer beware").

For purely selfish reasons, I am of course eager to meet other emergees who have *been there and done that emergee thing.* Until those meetings take place, I am comforted by the fact that the world is full of submergees. I know that, eventually, many submergees will make the decision that it is time for them to emerge, and then the exodus will have begun in earnest. We who are emergees will have a unique experience in common. As submergees and emergees, we will have reasons to rejoice, but we will also be marked by the unique sadness of our past.

I am not offering submergee adults a blanket endorsement for an emergee transition as a means to overcome their problems. I am not a counselor, medical doctor, or a mental health professional who is qualified to make recommendations for others. If anything, I am attempting to help prevent personal and relational tragedies by offering strong cautions for those who might act precipitously, while also sharing my unique experience in the clearest terms possible. The information I can share is limited and preliminary, but I trust that soon there will be many sources of help for submergees and others who care about this issue. With time, the situation can only get better.

Without a diagnostic and therapeutic resource base to rely upon for assistance, those who wish to emerge as well as those who need therapeutic help to deal with their existing submergee issues will need to be patient as pioneering research work and resource development is begun and eventually comes on line. In my case, I gained real strength from my faith that God was at work in my life, giving me His peace and guiding my steps. Because of the lonely and frightening nature of my experience, I readily admit that faith played a critical part in the success of my emergee journey. There will be much good that will come from putting an end to the submergee madness, but given the early state of our understandings, we will need to have a healthy dose of patience, humility, humor, and faith that the dark history of ignorance is going to eventually come to an end.

In the final analysis, the submergee boogieman is really a paper tiger. Once we have a clear picture of how foolish the creation of submergee children really is, we'll be able to laugh at ourselves, learn from our mistakes and make the changes we need to in order to put an end to our silliness. Giving this story names and faces will help to put our fears into perspective as we engage this cultural and social issue and solve it. For those who have to cope with the consequences of being intimately associated with submergees, or for submergees who seek to find healing by taking the emergee path as adults, the story will go on in a new way.

FINDING HEALING ~ CHAPTER 16

I have learned that success is to be measured not so much by the position that one has reached in life as much as by the obstacles which he has overcome while trying to succeed.

Booker T. Washington.

What can be said in response to submergees who want to know more about the doors of healing that opened up to me, as I learned about them in the course of my emergee journey? In order to do justice to that subject, I would need to begin another book that I am not currently qualified to write. I did write a chapter in which I attempted to give just such a meaningful response, but the early draft proved to be very detailed and somewhat boring. Instead of going on needlessly, I'll pass on a few quick comments that I hope will be helpful.

I have been warned that some would attack me for sharing the topics covered in *Hidden Handedness*. Their thinking is that the topic is controversial, and worse still, there's a risk that some who read this book might decide to follow in my footsteps without proper preparation and professional support. An example given is the sometimes stressful confusion in laterality that drivers traveling through countries with different lane controls can experience (e.g. US right side versus UK left side driving). *Isn't it true that people might experience similar confusion or worse as a consequence of reading your book and then deciding to emerge?* they ask. The answer is *Yes they might!*

For those who question the wisdom of sharing the story of submergees and emergees, I am prepared to ask questions too. *Is that kind of ignorance really bliss? Will pretending that a problem doesn't exist make it go away? What's your idea? Shall we prevent people from traveling to countries and driving because the lane laws are reversed? Or, how about disease? Shall we prevent visits to foreign lands, because travelers might be exposed to exotic and sometimes deadly diseases?* Now that I've told the story of submergees and emergees, I've shared information that can be used to put an end to ignorance. Our real problem isn't the wound: it is our inability to see it. In spite of my words of support for potential emergees, I will offer some parting advice to anyone who might consider the emergee journey: *proceed at your own risk - **caution advised!***

On my own short list of important helps, I have mentioned cursive copying exercises as the therapeutic activity that helped me the most. I still engage in that discipline as I find that I need it and as time permits. The joy of rediscovering a fluent hand that I get from these exercises remains as strong as ever. I also find that cursive copying just for the pleasure of reconnecting to this pure experience of handedness helps to encourage and calm me. Invariably, if I am in need of a time of quiet artistic experience, I find that a thirty or forty-five minute copying session pays off nicely. Other avenues that have helped me include lap swimming, sketching, and any form of exercise that enables concentration on body movement. I prefer to do things that enable the kind of meditative focus that increases awareness of the two sides of the body and mind working in harmony.

Examples of gaining pleasure from exercises that integrate body and mind and support emergee function can be found in activities as simple as switching sidedness by changing hands when eating, driving or shaving. There is a wonderful *difference* that comes to mind in these quiet moments of movement and observation. Observing the changes in one's body and mind that result when one hand works while the other one supports that work is a valuable exercise. Playing with the differences in sensation that can be experienced directly by deliberately alternating between one state of laterality and the other is downright fun, and a great chance to learn!

The joy of juggling objects such as a set of keys from hand to hand, of shooting baskets with a piece of waste paper, and the daily surprise of little details that come from being more aware of life processes all help to keep the reality of emerging tangible for me. For those who wanted more details, this *interior monologue* could easily extend to book length, but I'll spare you the recital of history and leave you to imagine how the few examples I've shared have played out in thousands of different ways.

For the sake of those who are candidates for the emergee journey, we need to have readily accessible and appropriate assessment and support tools in place. Prospective emergees really should have access to qualified professionals who can participate in the process of evaluation and treatment. If a positive diagnosis is made and one accepts the label of submergee, then an appropriate and acceptable course of action needs to be charted. If therapy is called for, then a prognosis of the individual's probable outcome would be helpful, so that intelligent decisions can be made by the submergee and his immediate support group. If an emergee process is initiated, there should be appropriate safeguards in place, regular evaluation, and case management protocols established that will help smooth the process out for the emergee in the event that difficulties are encountered.

Having read this book, you know the current answer to the question: *Where are the resources that submergees need?* To the best of my knowledge, we are years away from having the tools and resources we need to respond to submergee children or adults in a qualified manner. It is an exciting possibility that the body of work already completed by Sattler and her associates may provide a strong boost to the cause of submergees once it becomes accessible in languages other than German. If access to a developed body of resources for submergees is combined with an interest in helping submergees at a global level, the work done by Sattler could be priceless. Of interest to educators, Sattler's group has been active in curriculum revisions in the Province of Bavaria. There have also been efforts to revise educational practices relative to handedness in England and India and there may be many other individuals and groups I am not yet aware of that have been organized to help end submergee training in homes and elementary schools.

The submergee problem represents a tremendous and in some ways dangerous obstacle to overcome. I share the information in *Hidden Handedness* with real caution, knowing that some might not understand the legitimate concerns I have for submergees who could suffer negative consequences should they choose to embark on their own emergee journey without appropriate professional evaluation and support. I am not a trained professional, counselor or medical professional nor am I qualified to give advice. I am very concerned that the information I have shared be used responsibly given the limited amount that we now know about this topic. In the absence of others who can speak with more authority, I have chosen to tell my story. However, I must warn the reader that there are potential dangers and pitfalls for anyone who wishes to become an emergee pioneer.

Although submergees have been created in ignorance, we have a moral responsibility to work together to put an end to the process that continues to create submergees. We live in a world that is populated by adult submergees, a world that will continue to create young submergees who will grow up and take their place until we choose to stop the trauma. It is up to us to use our new awareness to create a world filled with normal, not-submerged children, and adult submergees who are understood and treated with compassion. Speaking in general terms about moral responsibility may seem like a strange way to conclude a chapter written to submergees interested in finding healing help, but the healing process really can't begin properly until submergees are recognized and accepted. The most important step in the healing process is the first step of recognition and acceptance that we all need to take together.

MANY PATHWAYS HOME ~ CHAPTER 17

The road goes ever on and on
Down from the door where it began,
Now far ahead the Road has gone,
And I must follow, if I can,
Pursuing it with eager feet,
Until it joins some larger way
Where many paths and errands meet,
And whither then? I cannot say.

The words of Bilbo Baggins – in JRR Tolkien's *The Fellowship of the Ring*

Because I started life all over again at a late age, I shall always have the special joy of having been a child twice. I now see the new awareness that developed in me, as a result of growing up once again beginning at age forty-one, as a rare gift. I hope I shall never lose the clear sense that my journey through life is being made by a completely new person. The understanding that I am now someone else, an emergee, will never cease to astound me.

It is really impossible to put into words the essentials of a discovery process driven by a sense of wonder that never ends. The dynamics are captured by the idea of a complete change or transformation of one's body image undergone in adulthood. The choice of the hand used to open doors, brush one's teeth, handle knives and utensils, even the hand used to throw with, shapes and forms an altered body and mind that sets the stage for the development of a different self. As in fairy tales, where the characters are magically capable of shifting their shapes, the template of the body and mind is a working platform that normally helps to maintain the status quo of the existing systems. In the case of submergees and emergees, their uniquely revised selves evoke a

195

sense of mystery and wonder within, as they almost magically enable the process of significant transformation and shifting of the body and mind.

For me, the choice to change the image of my body and mind required focused effort, a commitment to learn new skills and hours of uninterrupted time to learn them well, such as the throwing motion, writing cursive script, or the serve used in the game of tennis. With time, however, I learned that a surprising number of new skills can be mastered nicely by the body and mind. Mastery of more complex movements was fueled by the curiosity of discovery and an intense desire to learn new skills.

As complex skills are mastered, they are stored away as a revised set of memories that makes use of these talents routine matters that need not require conscious effort and energy. This stored information also forms the basis of our body image. The same golfer who has worked hard to improve his game and become more competitive, also develops a revised body image relating to golf, an image that is different than the body image he visualized when thinking of himself as a not-so-skilled golfer. While it is true that the range of areas where learning must take place is much more universal in an emergee, the same process is actually at work in the golfer, too.

Keep in mind that when a dominant hand is chosen, the full body follows suit, because the platform for movement of the hand is grounded in the supporting systems of the body and mind. I had always wondered, for example, why my basketball shots weren't more powerful and accurate. I had always felt that I had to shove or push the ball, instead of shooting with my whole body in the graceful and more accurate manner of normal players. The answer to my question came when I realized that the symphony of body movements that occur without conscious thought are initiated by the earliest shooting movements. These early movements set the optimal sequences into motion, mobilizing far more than just the arms and hands. As a submergee, I was missing the benefit of an integrated body and mind, thus my shots lacked the fluid transfer of force that enables the athletic accuracy and ease of movement that I now enjoy.

The demonstration of this whole body system of movement can easily be seen in the coordinated throwing motion of a baseball player who has a powerful arm, or in the fluid explosion of energy that is required to produce an outstanding tennis serve or a long drive in the game of golf. As the body supports movement of the hands, so the neurology that coordinates the hands is connected to the nervous system that serves the rest of the body. Neurological scans of these interrelated systems at work in the brain clearly show that *many* sites are employed in a coordinated concert that enables complex skills. Since skilled uses of the hands are necessary for so many human functions, altering the hemisphere that drives these communities of coordinated functions by switching dominant handedness represents a massive shift of organization within the body and mind. Seen as a coordinated set of interrelated systems, the sense of what an emergee return actually accomplishes becomes much easier to appreciate.

In The Creation of Adam, Michelangelo's fresco on the ceiling of the Sistine Chapel, God touches Adam's finger in order to endow Adam's body with life. This image of God touching man on the finger of his left hand captures someone of infinite potential connecting with the limited body and mind of man. The consequence of this divine union was animation and life, summoned forth from that which was inanimate. This picture also evokes the power of transformation that is resident in the body and mind because of life experiences. Like Michelangelo's Adam, we too are in many ways inanimate and helpless, but a fabulous capacity for transformation exists within each of us, a potential which is embodied in our hands.

SYNTHESIS OF THE SENSES ~ MORE NEW WORLDS TO EXPLORE

While visiting with my blind chiropractor, I told him about the intense sensory pleasure that I had felt in observing a woman standing in front of me in a checkout line, as she very mindfully touched a few items in her purse. As I watched her hands absentmindedly, I became aware of the manner in which this woman used her hands in a sensuous and almost erotic way. As I shared the profound nature of this experience with him, my chiropractor smiled knowingly and informed me that I was experiencing what he thought of as a synthesis of the senses, what he referred to as *multi-sensory perception*. I found his insight wonderfully comforting as he went on to explain that this kind of sensory integration and awareness is a pathway that adds richness to the sensory experiences of those who are blind. These late-developing experiences, or better still, *synthesized senses* have opened up new perceptual worlds to me, adding fresh depth and richness to life.

As the essentials of *being in* or being grounded and comfortably oriented in my own body were mastered, the avenues to multi-sensory development beckoned ahead. Traveling down the emergee river led me to an increasing number of opportunities for development, a larger set of possibilities that came into play through integration and synthesis. The larger implications of multi-sensory experience are that it is possible to more fully inhabit the senses, to become completely at home in the real body and mind, a fact which in turn evokes the potential to become more fully alive to all of the senses. Multi-sensory perception opens up a host of complex and rich sensations that involve all of the senses, and the synthesis of these senses into fresh frameworks of perception that can link and connect emergees and others more intensely to the world of experiences.

To get a sense of the concepts of revised body image and multi-sensory experiences, try using your non-dominant hand to write in cursive style for five minutes or more, long enough to get a sense of *inhabiting* your sub-dominant hand in a meaningful way. Does the process of focusing on that hand evoke a feeling of being strange or somehow different? In a simplified sense, emerging consists of overcoming that kind of alienation. The emergee must eventually learn to live more comfortably, to be more at home in the strange hand than in the hand which had once been dominant. In my case, my left hand had to become the hand I really preferred to use when given a choice for skilled uses such as cursive writing.

Having used your non-dominant hand for a few minutes, now pick up the same writing instrument with your dominant hand and as you do, imagine that this comfortable use were possible with the other hand too. If that kind of skill and ease of use were to suddenly be transferred to your non-dominant hand, you might choose to become ambidextrous or even to emerge yourself upon realizing that skills that surpass those of the dominant hand are accessible when using your non-dominant hand. If you are reading these comments as a submergee, you might have the privilege of considering this option in terms of a life-long change.

For the emergee, this kind of an unexpected *experience of difference* in capacity between the hands, which you may have just enacted, takes place in an even more intense manner. Changing the behavior of the body and mind by behaving in accord with a revised self-image can have a profound impact on one's identity, the very seat of the body and mind. This happens in the emergee because the transition occurs not only in their hands, but also in all of their other systems over a period of many years, starting with basic senses, opening up multi-sensory perceptions and even the manner in which thinking takes place, the thought process. To illustrate the depth to which this revised self-image affected me, after eleven years of life as an emergee, I recently saw a right-handed colleague writing with his right hand and it occurred to me that it seemed strange that he wasn't using his left hand!

THE HIDDEN HARVEST

The fact that I had passed the unexpected developmental milestone of multi-sensory awareness came as a very pleasant surprise. The net effect or harvest of multi-sensory integration was an improved personal and social awareness that further opened up the avenues of social commerce. The emerging ability to better appreciate oneself and others, to more deeply sense their feelings and inner states, and to also participate more completely in the interactions that come from relationships depends upon a healthy ripening of myriads of systems in the body and mind. For me, this ripening was a much delayed but intensely meaningful process. The critical human skills that join us in healthy social bonds are either enhanced or degraded by the presence or absence of an integrated multi-sensory awareness that enables us to perceive ourselves and others as fully as possible.

I would say that gaining greater access to the multi-sensory *benefit of a more fully developed awareness* represents a hidden harvest of the emergee experience. This was the icing on the multi-layered cake that I first began to experience after some five years of living as an emergee. This more fine-grained awakening has proven to be as important to the healing process as access to writing therapy and enhanced neurological function were in the first months of the experience. These subtle yet rich late multi-sensory awakenings continue as I mature and find, over time, that the ability to love and relate to self and others grows richer and deeper.

THAWING OUT

I would compare my emotional awakening to the feeling that comes when blood returns to an arm or leg that has been numb. I experienced a gradual warming and sense of emotional life in a part of my self that had been numb. If my experience proves true for other emergees, one of the long-term payoffs for those who are willing to assist the emergee to grow up will come as the emergee begins to gain better access to emotions. Their improved sense of interconnection, and the many sensory and multi-sensory pathways they will learn to access, will eventually enable them to connect more completely to themselves, and then to those that they love.

In the physical realm, formation of the new habits of body and mind that resulted in a more comfortable seat of self took all of five years to happen. I judge this comfort level every time I pick up a pen and write. If I am comfortably at home in my body and attending to the writing process, the pen feels natural and my writing feels easy in the same way that walking does. There are other moments when I experience a momentary sense of awkwardness, which I can mindfully overcome or ignore. I have learned to be thankful for these reminders of my past, because each time as I begin to write fluidly with my left hand, a warm sense of joy comes, as I am reminded that I am now free from my submergee prison. I can be the person that I was designed to be in spite of my submergee past.

On a more somber note, I find the knowledge that I came close to losing my life due to my own struggles with depression rather frightening. I could have easily become a suicide statistic on at least three occasions prior to my emergee experience. Now that the undertow and relentless downward suction of my submergee deficits are gone, I have effectively escaped from the dull dragging forces I once struggled against. Although I no longer suffer from chronic depression, I am deeply touched by the pain and struggles of submergees and others who do. Because of the wonderful relief from depression that I found in my emergee recovery, I am very hopeful that a better understanding of the problem will result from future clinical work with submergees and emergees. Research into the neurology of submergees as well as emergees may hold a key that will help to unlock fresh insights into the causes of depression that may help to bring healing to those who suffer from its horrors.

Temple Grandin's wonderful book *Seeing In Pictures* vividly expresses something of the emergee experience that I have described in this book as she writes about what it meant to begin recovering from her autistic deficits. Note that in her case, too, a combination of developmental accomplishments culminated in significant changes, alterations in her body and mind that others were able to recognize.

Even though I felt relief immediately after I started the drug, [sic: as a therapy for the physiological struggles that came as a consequence of autism] however, my behavior changed slowly. There were obvious improvements that everybody noticed immediately, but over the years there have been more subtle gains. For instance, many people who have attended my lectures for some time have noticed that they keep getting smoother and better. An old friend whom I hadn't seen in seven years, since I started taking medication, informed me that I now walked with my back straight rather than hunched up. I had stopped walking with a limp and seemed like a completely different person to her. I know that I had sometimes hunched, but never realized that I used to sound like I was always catching my breath or that I was constantly swallowing. My eye contact had also improved, and I no longer had a shifty eye. People report that they now have a more personal feeling when they talk to me.[53]

A critical difference between the emergee process and the experiences described by Grandin is the fact that there is no need for drug therapy in order for the submergee to become whole. Ending the cycle of submergee entrapment begins where it started, by opening and passing through the very door of handedness expression that was once slammed shut. Temple Grandin and others have written about their experiences and in doing so, they have given me great encouragement, a sense of the larger community of people who are connected in some manner to submergees and emergees.

In time, individuals who have Asperger's Syndrome, those with autism, dyslexia and a host of other *isms* will no doubt discover much in common with submergees and emergees in ways that we can't begin to understand now. My hope is that in a few more years, new therapeutic avenues and research insights will light up and secure the pathways we need to travel on as we find our way home. As we learn more about submergees and emergees, I believe that this coming home, the understanding and acceptance of one hidden part of humanity, will result in a harvest of blessings that will open doors of healing for all of us.

This is a time when we need explorers, those who are willing to set sail into the bourgeoning world of body and mind research. Precisely because we are awash in a growing sea of information and insights, we need heroines and heroes who are willing to do the hard work of sailing forth, navigating, exploring, and ultimately making sense of our dazzling and newly accessible inner worlds. Submergees and emergees may well play a leading role in the journeys of understanding and learning that lay before us. My hope is that we shall learn what it means to explore the limitless horizons that lay ahead with fresh abandon, and that submergees and emergees will add new resources and insights to our quest.

END

APPENDIX A

August 4, 1999

Oliver Sacks, MD
2 Horatio St. 3G
New York, NY 10014

Dear Dr. Sacks,

I have a story that you may wish to know about. You may be familiar with the events that I relate in this letter. If you are, it would be a great pleasure to hear back from you or others who have had the same experience. I was born in the fall of 1952 and somewhere between 12 and 18 months, my mother tells me that I was identified as a left-handed child by my left-handed grandmother. Thus began the process of training a left-handed child to become a right-handed child. I was never told that this retraining had happened. What followed was the predictable; learning disabilities associated with dyslexia, mirror writing as well as poor academic and athletic performance. In second grade, I was diagnosed by a developmental optometrist as suffering from lazy eye, but the therapy recommended by the OD wasn't administered. I grew up with all of the experiences that learning disabled children are familiar with, knowing that I was "slow" in comparison to my older and younger brothers.

In 1984, I finally realized that I was a "compensated dyslexic" after reading the book *Smart But Feeling Dumb* written by Harold N. Levinson MD The understanding that followed this primary insight was very helpful, although the experience of having to constantly overcome or compensate for hearing, academic and mental hurdles was something I was aware of. Then in January of

1995, I remember praying and asking the question *Why must I live in a retarded state of mind?* At the time, I felt as though I was given an answer that I could accept with a certain sense of peace and was willing to accept my fate for the balance of my life.

However, on March 5, 1995, less than three months later, I can only say in retrospect that God *opened my eyes* and revealed to me that I was actually left-handed. At the time, I had no idea that this insight would in some way connect to my prayer for deliverance from mental bondage some three moths prior. The insight that broke the noose occurred as I was playing tennis against a backboard on that date. Because I was unable to "charge the boards successfully" playing right-handed, I switched hands and suddenly found that I was able to remain "on" the ball and charge the wall successfully. For some reason, my brain noted that the sound pattern of my footsteps changed, or was "an organized set of squeaks" when I played with the racquet in my left hand and a "disorganized set of squeaks" when I played with the racquet in my right hand.

This process of discovery continued as I arrived at home, explained my new convictions to my wife of 9 plus years and was given her full endorsement. When I shared my insight, my wife confessed that she already knew that I was a lefty, because she had heard a radio program some months earlier in which psychologist Donald Joy, PhD had been interviewed and discussed individuals who suffered from what he referred to as anomalous dominance, a phenomenon or state of being associated with switched lefties. Further, my parents admitted that my surmise was correct, that I was a left-handed individual and that in fact, my father was also a switched lefty.

Not knowing the changes that were to follow my discovery, I simply accepted the new knowledge and began to behave accordingly by becoming fully left-handed. I began copying in cursive form from 1 to 3 hours per day and I began living by using my left hand as the dominant hand. I have kept a dated record of the copying work as well as my journal of the changes which is current to this date. What has happened in the days, weeks and months since that beginning can only be described as a "neurological resurrection from the dead." The strangest part of the resurrection however, is the very weird experience of learning that apparently, no one else has had the same experience. If they have, they haven't written about it, and no one I have checked with has a record of this experience of switching one's assumed and "natural" dominance.

For a sense of the experience I am sharing with you, I recently was traveling and drove past a van filled with children affected with Down's Syndrome. That sight of those young people was an overwhelming emotional experience for me, because I too, was mentally and emotionally in a very similar state until age 41. I just appeared normal to others. Today, I would report that I am a fully functional human, totally free of the burdens of "dyslexia". I am no longer riding in anyone's van for the disabled.

I could easily bore you with the details of the changes that followed the discovery of March 5, 1995. It has been 4 years and 5 months since my left-handed birthday. In that interim, I have prepared the rough draft for a book about the experience, but have had zero success in locating an agent who would like to help publish the story to date. As you might imagine, I feel a tremendous burden to get the news out to what must be a population of millions like me, who aren't free, who are walking through life as right-handed zombies, when a pathway to full function is available to every one of them. If only they knew. However, the information must be shared in a responsible manner, so that the spin offs of "becoming another person at an adult age" don't create tragic and destructive waves in the relationships that they have with themselves and just as importantly, those who love them, and must adjust and participate in the process I have very briefly described.

Based on the little I now know about you, (two movies and several articles as well as the information on your website) I believe that you are probably the best person available to tell the story that needs to be told. I did meet with Dr. Levinson some three years ago and he did indicate serious interest in researching the topic as it relates to his focus on dyslexia. He was particularly interested in this drug-free cure for the malady. Unfortunately, he has been too busy with his own practice to tackle the research project to date. Although I am convinced that the subject of anomalous dominance merits research, and would be of great interest, the immediate need is to tell the story to as many people as possible. You may have other insights regarding timing and the need for research that I would be very interested to hear. In any case, I have resolved to do what I must do in order to get this story told, but the question is, what can one person do and how many years will it take for the news to reach those that it could benefit?

I can assure you that the prejudices that force hand switches are alive and well today. This is a global issue that could set millions of people free from bondage. Donald Joy estimates that the academic penalty for switching is 1.5 grade points. I would concur. Imagine that the following <u>permanent</u> improvements were to occur in even one percent of the world's switched population and imagine that the process which creates the problem were to be discontinued altogether:

Listing of changes noted upon exiting from AD state

Major improvements in visual acuity
Major improvements in auditory acuity
Major improvement in memory
Increased emotional depth
Increased depth of humor
Improved spelling
Improved grammar
Improved math skills
Enhanced academic skills
Enhanced artistic skills
Improved interpersonal and social skills
Improved body posture
Improved body image
Improved body health - 6 hours of sleep needed when 8 were needed before

Improved athletic ability (I am a lap swimmer, ask me about Finesse Technique sometime)

In January of this year, I finally came to the place where I realized that I was ready to share the story at a public level. Those I discuss the subject with "light up" with understanding of the importance of the topic because I think I am now able to express the subject of handedness switches in a meaningful way to others. The number of people who are either interested in or related to someone that the issue touches is more significant than I had thought. It was in January of this year that I made the decision to begin the process of sharing my experience in the public forum. Shortly thereafter, I learned about your work. After learning what I have about your interest area, I think that you may be a perfect fit for this subject area. If the subject were to interest you, and if it were presented successfully, the changed lives of those who benefited could provide a suitable framework for the work you have done to date in drawing humanity's attention to the sleeping mind and its potential once it has been set free of unnecessary limits.

I look forward to your response.

Samuel M. Randolph

(Note - letter edited for grammatical errors and reprinted)

APPENDIX B

GLOSSARY OF TERMS USED

Alter - short for alter personality. A term which is commonly used in connection with Dissociative Identity Disorder (DID) or Multiple Personality Disorder (MPD).

Body Image. (both meanings are used)

1. Is a person's perception of his or her physical appearance. A person with a poor body image will perceive their own body as being unattractive or even repulsive to others. While a person with good body image, or positive "body acceptance", will either see themselves as attractive to others, or will at least accept it as is. Body image is most strongly affected during puberty.

2. There is another technical use of the term "body image" which refers to the association of areas of the motor cortex with the voluntary movement of body members. This is often shown as the motor homunculus depicted by Dr. Wilder Penfield. This image distorts the body according to the areas of the motor cortex associated with its movements. For example it shows the thumb as larger than the thigh because the thumb's movement is much more complex than that of the thigh and thus occupies a larger area of the cortex than the thigh. The motor homunculus plays a central role in proprioception, i.e. our actual perception of being embodied. This body-image is involved in phantom limb phenomena and their opposite as in the case of brain damage resulting in the disappearance of parts of the body from conscious perception.

Source: Wikipedia, The Free Encyclopedia.
http://en.wikipedia.org/wiki/Body_image.

Interhemispheric Transfer Times (ITT). A measure of reaction speed which compares the transfer rate (speed) of signal processing as measured by movement in response to a stimulus with particular reference to the transfer of information between hemispheres via the connecting pathway of the corpus callosum.

Submergee. An individual who as a child was trained by others, or convinced to train themselves to function using their non preferred hand as if it were their dominant hand. Typically, a left-handed child is taught or trained to function as a right-handed child, particularly in the act of writing. The reverse process of training a right-handed child to become left-handed can and does also occur. Normally, the process of becoming a submergee takes place over many years as the altered habits of submergee behavior are formed and assimilated as if they were the normal behaviors of the submergee.

Emergee. A submergee child or adult who recognizes their submergee status and decides to return to their native handedness.

Normal submergee. A submergee adult or child who can recall the trauma of being forced to reverse their handedness or having been convinced that reversing their handedness and becoming a submergee would be their wisest course of action, one that would serve their best interests.

Deep submergee. A submergee adult or child who cannot recall the trauma of being forced to reverse their handedness or having been convinced that reversing their handedness and becoming a submergee would serve their best interests.

Conservation of mind. In the context of submergee function, the utilization of the formerly non-dominant hemisphere for primary motor function would normally result in a loss of neurons in the dormant hemisphere where the weight of function was once primary. The term conservation is used, because those neurological resources and skills that would normally be removed through neural pruning, or reallocated to other uses are conserved, rather than lost in this transition. Strong evidence supporting the notion that conservation of mind is at work in enabling submergee function and the emergee recovery comes from both PET imaging of submergee subjects engaged in writing with their right hand and observed rebound effects, in which cognitive and physiological functions are enhanced rather than degraded by an emergee return.

Dissociative Identity Disorder (DID) and Multiple Personality Disorder (MPD). In psychiatry, Dissociative Identity Disorder (DID) is the current name of the condition formerly listed in the Diagnostic and Statistical Manual of Mental Disorders as Multiple Personality Disorder (MPD) and Multiple Personality Syndrome. The International Statistical Classification of Diseases and Related Health Problems continues to list it as Multiple Personality Disorder. Multiple Personality Disorder should not be confused with schizophrenia.

According to standard American textbooks in clinical psychology, Dissociative Identity Disorder is a psychological condition characterized by the use of dissociation as a primary defense mechanism. A chronic reliance on dissociation as a means of defending against stressors in the environment causes the individual to experience their psyche/identity as disconnected or split into distinct parts.

Source - Wikipedia The Free Encyclopedia
http://en.wikipedia.org/wiki/Dissociative_identity_disorder. See this source for a more complete discussion and references.

END NOTES

Chapter 1

1. The focus on handwriting as "the" identifying feature is admittedly simplistic, because there are many ingredients at work and many variables to consider in the larger context of laterality. However, since handedness is the single most popular target for reversal attempts, and since handwriting can be studied in historical documents and in photographs, it makes an ideal starting point in the study of handedness reversals. Porac and Friesen state that "The results shown . . . confirm previous reports that hand preference switch attempts target specific behaviors, usually the rightward switch of the writing hand, leaving other behaviors unaffected and with continued left-hand preference . . ." (Porac, 1996a; Porac et al., 1990) as cited in Developmental Neurophysiology 17: 236. Coren states that "The most common activity targeted for change was writing, as we had suspected." page 68 *The Left-Hander Syndrome: The Causes And Consequences Of Left-Handedness* by Stanley Coren.

2. Until recently, for one to claim that handedness reversals result in a specific alteration in brain function would be impossible to support with direct evidence. However, research published in the Journal of Neuroscience April 1, 2002 shows the unique neurological signature of those subjects whose handedness had been reversed. PET scans of these subjects clearly showed that when the submergee subjects were engaged in a writing task, abnormal use of the sub-dominant hemisphere takes place. See LONG-TERM CONSEQUENCES OF SWITCHING HANDEDNESS: A POSITRON EMISSION TOMOGRAPHY STUDY ON HANDWRITING IN "CONVERTED" LEFT-HANDERS 22: 2816-2825.

3. Three of the more fascinating examples of this experience are

212

submergee Jack Fincher who wrote *Lefties - The Origins & Consequences of Being Left-Handed*, submergee Eileen Simpson, author of *Reversals: A Personal Account Of Victory Over Dyslexia* and deep submergee Bernard Selling. Selling writes about his experience in *Writing from Within: A Guide to Creativity and Life Story Writing*. Of the three, the most dramatic case is that of Simpson, who went on to become a practicing psychotherapist. In spite of the fact that Simpson clearly relates the painful details of her submergee training and the experiences that followed, she remains trapped in her submergee experience and struggles with dyslexia.

4. IBID. For those who are interested in further reading sources, both the written works and personal notes of known submergees can serve as a resource. One example is the recently published book containing the letters of submergee President Ronald Reagan. See *Reagan: A Life In Letters by Kiron K. Skinner*.

5. Studies completed by Marian Annette, psychologist and researcher at the University of Leichester, England and extensive work by other researchers interested in the laterality of humans have shown that an approach to laterality which is based on varying degrees of handedness or "strengths" of handedness provides us with a model that closely fits research data from a wide range of research. Annette's model plots the strength of handedness on a bell curve. Based on the logic of this model, those who are most strongly handed are placed toward the outer ends, or thin ends of the bell curve. The vertical axis which is placed on the curve to define ambidexterity is "shifted" to the left of center in order to account for the asymmetry of human handedness, in which roughly 90% of humans are thought to be right-handed, leaving a remainder of some 10% who are thought to be left-handed. The 90/10 ratio of handedness varies due to culture, sex and age, but the notion that handedness is manifested in individuals in varying degrees or *strengths* remains constant.

Chapter 6

6. *Hands* - article by Oliver Sacks - The New York Review of Books, November 8, 1984.

Chapter 7

7. Ratey, John J. MD (2002) *A User's Guide to the Brain: Perception, Attention, and the Four Theaters of the Brain.* Page 55. New York. Vintage Books.

8. VOLUNTARY CONTROL OF TWO LATERALIZED CONSCIOUS STATES: VALIDATION BY ELECTRICAL AND BEHAVIORAL STUDIES. Peggy S Gott, Everett C. Hughes and Katherine Whipple. Neuropsychologia Vol. 22, No 1. pp 65-72 1984.

9. INTERHEMISPHERIC TRANSFER OF COLOR CUES. BRAIN AND LANGUAGE 73, 245-273 (2000). Available online at www.idealibrary.com.

In an update on the topic of interhemispheric transfers, German researchers using pigeons as subjects studied the mechanisms that mediate interhemispheric asymmetry. The report cites findings in humans reported in separate studies completed by Marzi et al. (1991), Novicka et al (1996), and Nalcaci et al. (1999) that found evidence of established asymmetry in the ITT of human subjects.

In the concluding comments of their paper titled INTERHEMISPHERIC TRANSFER OF COLOR CUES, which represents an update on the topic of interhemispheric transfer mechanisms and ITT, the report reads as follows ". . . Taken together, these results suggest that asymmetries of interhemispheric transfer may be a widespread phenomenon which could represent a key principle in the maintenance of lateralizations."

The same report also states that ". . . After the end of this transient period, [during which time the asymmetry of a pigeon's visual system is established] the established asymmetries determine the lateralized processes of the visual system *for the entire life span of the individual.*" (emphasis mine).

10. An excellent reference source on DID is the book *The Stranger In the Mirror, Dissociation - The Hidden Epidemic*. Marlene Steinberg, MD and Maxine Schanall (2000) Harper Collins Books, New York, NY. For a detailed case study of DID (which is referred to as Multiple Personality Disorder in the following study) and its connection to handedness and laterality, see CONDITIONAL HANDEDNESS: HANDEDNESS CHANGES IN MULTIPLE PERSONALITY DISORDERED SUBJECT REFLECT SHIFT IN HEMISPHERIC DOMINANCE by Polly Henninger. Consciousness and Cognition 1, 265-287, 1992.

11. Journal of Neuroscience April 1, 2002. LONG-TERM CONSEQUENCES OF SWITCHING HANDEDNESS: A POSITRON EMISSION TOMOGRAPHY STUDY ON HANDWRITING IN "CONVERTED" LEFT-HANDERS 22: 2816-2825.

12. Ratey, John J. MD (2002) *A User's Guide to the Brain: Perception, Attention, and the Four Theaters of the Brain*. Page 38. New York. Vintage Books.

Chapter 8

13. Oliver Sacks MD (11/3/84) *Hands*. The New York Review of Books

Chapter 10

14. Coren, Stanley (1992). *The Left-Hander Syndrome: The Causes And Consequences Of Left-Handedness*. Page 68. New York, NY: Random House, Inc.

15. Miller et al. (3/22/2000) INTERHEMISPHERIC SWITCHING MEDIATES PERCEPTUAL RIVALRY. Current Biology 2000 10: 383-392

16. Andrew Newberg of the University of Pennsylvania, the author of *Why God Won't Go Away: Brain Science and the Biology of Belief.* Comments excerpted from *God & The Brain* Newsweek May 7, 2001. Interview with Dr. Andrew Newberg Univ. of Pennsylvania.

17. Simpson, Eileen (1998) *Reversals: A Personal Account of Victory over Dyslexia.* Pg. 25 The Noonday Press.

18. Fincher, Jack (1993) *Lefties - The Origins & Consequences Of Being Left-Handed.* Pages 19-20. Barnes & Noble Books. New York, NY.

19. Selling, Bernard (1998) *Writing from Within: A Guide to Creativity and Life Story Writing.* Page 111. Hunter House Inc., Publishers, Alameda, CA.

Chapter 11

20. VanBuren, *Soft In The Heart.* Page 46. As cited by Jack Fincher (1993) in *Lefties - The Origins & Consequences Of Being Left-Handed.* Opening pages. Barnes & Noble Books. New York, NY.

Chapter 12

21. Coren, Stanley (1992). *The Left-Hander Syndrome: The Causes And Consequences Of Left-Handedness.* Page 1. New York, NY: Random House, Inc.

22. Morris, Edmund (1999) *Dutch - A Memoir of Ronald Reagan.* Page 93. Random House, New York, NY.

23. IBID.

24. John Hutton Diary, August 27, 1987, JHP.

25. Morris, Edmund (1999) *Dutch - A Memoir of Ronald Reagan* page 93. Random House, New York, NY. End notes of Edmund Morris on President Reagan's left-handedness referenced to page 93.

26. IBID - see pages referenced.

27. IBID. This quote of Morris appears on the fly leaf of the book.

28. IBID. see page 318.

29. Regan, Donald, T. *For The Record* (1988) - From Wall Street to Washington pages 276-277. St Martin's Press, New York, N.Y.

30. Robins, Charles, *Last Of His Kind* (1979) - An Informal Portrait of Harry S. Truman page 146. William Morrow and Company Inc. New York, N.Y.

31. McManus, Chris (2002) *Right Hand Left Hand: The Origins of Asymmetry In Brains, Bodies, Atoms And Cultures.* Harvard University Press. Cambridge, Massachusetts.

32. IBID page 300.

Chapter 13

33. Geyer, Georgie Anne (2001) *Guerrilla Prince: The Untold Story of Fidel Castro.* Andrews McMeel Publishing, Kansas City.

34. IBID. Introduction, page XXIV-XXV.

35. IBID. Introduction, page XXI-XXIII.

Chapter 14

36. Coren, Stanley (1992). *The Left-Hander Syndrome: The Causes And Consequences Of Left-Handedness.* Page 263. New York, NY: Random House, Inc.

37. Coren, Stanley (1992). *The Left-Hander Syndrome: The Causes And Consequences Of Left-Handedness.* Page 262. New York, NY: Random House, Inc.

38. The term "Inner Critic" was coined by authors Hal and Sidra Stone. See their book, *Embracing Your Inner Critic: Turning Self-*

Criticism Into A Creative Asset for further discussion.

39. Coren, Stanley (1992). *The Left-Hander Syndrome: The Causes And Consequences Of Left-Handedness.* Pages 68-69. New York, NY: Random House, Inc.

40. McManus, Chris (2002). *Right Hand Left Hand: The Origins of Asymmetry In Brains, Bodies, Atoms And Cultures* Page 300. Cambridge, Massachusetts. Harvard University Press.

41. Coren, Stanley (1992). *The Left-Hander Syndrome: The Causes And Consequences Of Left-Handedness.* Pages 68-69. New York, NY: Random House, Inc.

42. Coren, Stanley (1992). *The Left-Hander Syndrome: The Causes And Consequences Of Left-Handedness.* Page 69. New York, NY: Random House, Inc.

43. Report of Steele and Mays summarized in their paper NEW FINDINGS ON THE FREQUENCY OF LEFT-AND RIGHT-HANDEDNESS IN MEDIEVAL BRITAIN. Steele & Mays. The comments which follow can be found that a web site maintained by James Steele: http://www.soton.ac.uk/~tjms/handed.html and in a reference a paper authored by Steele and Mays published in 1995 in the International Journal of Osteoarcheolgy 5:39-49 titled HANDEDNESS AND DIRECTIONAL ASYMMETRY IN THE LONG BONES OF THE HUMAN UPPER LIMB.

44. IBID.

45. Citation of work completed by Peter Hepper of the Queen's University of Belfast by Chris McManus McManus, Chris (2002) *Right Hand Left Hand: The Origins of Asymmetry In Brains, Bodies, Atoms And Cultures.* Page 156. Cambridge, Massachusetts. Harvard University Press.

46. VOLUNTARY CONTROL OF TWO LATERALIZED CONSCIOUS STATES: VALIDATION BY ELECTRICAL AND

BEHAVIORAL STUDIES published in Neuropsychologia Vol. 22 No. 1, pp. 65-72, 1984. Peggy S. Gott, Everett C. Hughes and Katherine Whipple.

Researchers at University of Southern California School of Medicine clinically evaluated a subject who demonstrated the capacity to voluntarily control or switch dominance from one hemisphere to the other. In the course of the study, the subject demonstrated shifts in her hemispheric dominance which were affirmed using both ITT and EEG alpha measurements. These measurements illustrated classic differences in the ITT efficiency of dominant versus sub-dominant hemispheres as expected, as well as differences in ITT that could be attributed to state-dependent shifts in the hemispheric dominance of the subject.

In order to verify the fact that a shift in lateralization had occurred using ITT data, measurement of differences in the reaction times of the subject to a given stimulus were made for each of the two states of hemispheric dominance. The differences in the reaction speeds measured when the fingers of contralateral and ipsilateral hands were stimulated gave researchers a means of correlating differences in the subject's ITT to her state-dependent shifts in dominance.

Using these test data as a reference point, it appears as if shifts of hemispheric dominance resulted in a rough equivalence of performance as documented by the ITT results which appear in figure 2 of the report. These results would seem to indicate that the characteristics of the voluntary shift of dominance which was studied by these researchers is distinct from the process which submergees experience. German researcher, Johanna Barbara Sattler, PhD, posits a loss in operating efficiency of between 30 to 300% in the brains of the submergees she has studied, a surmise which checks with my own observations and coincidentally, a support for the rebound phenomena experienced by emergees.

Based on this data, it would be appropriate to claim that a loss of operating efficiency (reaction speed) connected with processing signals originating from the non dominant hemisphere, such as that which was illustrated by the ITT testing cited would represent the minimal impact of a permanent shift to submergee status for a given individual. The fact that the subject of the study of the USC group could voluntarily control something as profound as her hemispheric dominance underscores the complex operational possibilities of the bilateral brain and the kind of mechanisms which enable submergee and emergee changes to occur. Studies such as this one also point to the urgent need for fresh research regarding the processes and underlying mechanisms that enable adaptations such as those which make submergee and emergee alterations possible in humans.

47. In an update on the topic of interhemispheric transfers, German researchers using pigeons as subjects studied the mechanisms the mediate interhemispheric asymmetry. The report cites findings in humans reported in separate studies completed by Marzi et al. (1991), Novicka et al (1996), and Nalcaci et al. (1999) that found evidence of established asymmetry in the ITT of human subjects.

In the concluding comments of their paper titled INTERHEMISPHERIC TRANSFER OF COLOR CUES, which represents an update on the topic of interhemispheric transfer mechanisms and ITT, the report reads as follows ". . . Taken together, these results suggest that asymmetries of interhemispheric transfer may be a widespread phenomenon which could represent a key principle in the maintenance of lateralizations."

The same report also states that ". . . After the end of this transient period, [during which time the asymmetry of a pigeon's visual system is established] the established asymmetries determine the lateralized processes of the visual system _for the entire life span of the individual._" (emphasis mine). See _Brain And Language_ 73, 254-273 (2000). Available on line at www.idealibrary.com

48. In a study published in Consciousness and Cognition 1, 265-287, 1992, Polly Henninger of Cal Tech reports on shifts in hemispheric dominance that are associated with shifts in personas.

The paper, titled CONDITIONAL HANDEDNESS: HANDEDNESS CHANGES IN MULTIPLE PERSONALITY DISORDERED SUBJECT REFLECT SHIFT IN HEMISPHERIC DOMINANCE.

49. *Wink Of An Eye.* Scientific American, May 1999. Pages 26-28. Jessa Netting.

50. Oliver Sacks, MD (1998) *A Leg To Stand On.* Pg 194 Touchstone, New York, NY.

51. Sperry, Roger - Public lecture presented at the Smithsonian Institution, December 1977, in the Frank Nelson Doubleday Lecture Series on THE HUMAN MIND

Chapter 15

52. Fincher, Jack (1993) *Lefties - The Origins & Consequences Of Being Left-Handed.* Page 21. Barnes & Noble Books. New York, NY.

53. Grandin, Temple (1995) *Thinking In Pictures And Other Reports From My Life With Autism. Pages* 116-117. Vintage Books, a division of Random House, Inc. New York, NY.

INDEX

A

academic deficits, 13, 26, 27
Annette, Marian, 8, 168, 169, 170, 213
Asian, 115, 170

B

behaviors, i, 27, 32, 55, 67, 78, 80, 85, 136, 137, 138, 140, 142, 153, 172, 210, 212
BIG TOE, 171
biography, 126, 127, 129, 131, 132, 134, 135, 145, 151, 153, 162
Bonaparte, Napoleon, 144

C

Castro, Fidel, 112, 149, 150, 151, 155, 156, 157, 217
changing handedness, 107
Conservation of mind, 210
Coren, Stanley, 107, 110, 115, 116, 119, 148, 155, 158, 160, 165, 167, 168, 212, 215, 216, 217, 218
culture, 76, 150, 159, 166, 167, 168, 170, 183, 185, 186, 213

D

depression, 11, 15, 98, 102, 125, 161, 162, 163, 182, 201
diagnostic tests, 144
Dissociative Identity Disorders, 79
dominant hand, 3, 76, 176, 196, 198, 199, 205, 210

E

emergee jump, 187, 188
emotional, 63, 86, 88, 89, 128, 130, 161, 178, 200, 206, 207

M

Mays, Simon, 169, 170, 218
McManus, Chris, 143, 144, 174, 217, 218
Morris, Edmund, 126, 127, 128, 129, 130, 131, 132, 133, 134, 135, 136, 137, 138, 139, 144, 145, 146, 147, 150, 151, 153, 216, 217
multi-sensory, 198, 199, 200

P

parents, 2, 11, 29, 35, 36, 37, 38, 51, 97, 99, 104, 121, 148, 149, 155, 183, 187, 205
PET scans, 81, 82, 84, 149, 212
politics, 112, 156, 157
population, 3, 119, 120, 121, 158, 164, 166, 167, 169, 170, 171, 183, 206, 207

R

Ratey, John, 71, 82, 83, 214, 215
Reagan, Ronald, 112, 126, 127, 128, 129, 130, 131, 132, 133, 134, 135, 136, 137, 138, 139, 140, 141, 142, 144, 145, 146, 147, 151, 155, 156, 157, 213, 216
rebound effect, 83, 173, 185
resources, 8, 56, 58, 69, 82, 83, 106, 107, 108, 113, 139, 143, 144, 151, 163, 173, 177, 180, 184, 185, 189, 193, 210
risk, 149, 186, 187, 188, 191, 192
Ritter, John, 13, 116

S

Sacks, Oliver, i, ii, 55, 86, 99, 107, 108, 116, 179, 204, 214, 215, 221
Sattler, Johanna Barbara, 185, 193, 219
school, 13, 15, 18, 19, 21, 22, 23, 26, 29, 36, 53, 98, 103, 125, 135, 155, 167, 184
Second Hand, 4, 5
Selling, Bernard, 115, 213, 216
Simpson, Eileen, 113, 114, 162, 213, 216
Sperry, Roger, 79, 110, 179
Springer, Sally P. and Deutsch, Georg, 108
Steele, James, 169, 170, 218

CPSIA information can be obtained at www.ICGtesting.com
Printed in the USA
LVOW13s1628290114

371500LV00002B/398/A